DANTE'S SECOND LOVE

The Originality and the Contexts of the Convivio

BY

PETER DRONKE

The Barlow Dante Lectures delivered at University College London 1–2 November 1995

OCCASIONAL PAPERS

NUMBER 2

Published by Routledge for
THE SOCIETY FOR ITALIAN STUDIES
1997

Routledge
Taylor & Francis Group
LONDON AND NEW YORK

PUBLISHED FOR
THE SOCIETY FOR ITALIAN STUDIES
BY ROUTLEDGE

2 Park Square, Milton Park, Abingdon, Oxfordshire OX14 4RN
52 Vanderbilt Avenue, New York, NY 10017

Routledge is an imprint of the Taylor & Francis Group, an informa business

First issued in paperback 2018

ISBN 13: 978-0-9525901-2-5 (pbk)

CONTENTS

	PREFACE	v
I	FROM BEATRICE TO THE DONNA GENTILE	1
II	THE DONNA GENTILE: *OBSCURIS VERA INVOLVENS*	26
III	'ETHICS AND AESTHETICS ARE ONE'	51
	EXCURSUS: THE 'REJECTION' OF THE DONNA GENTILE	72

PREFACE

In November 1995 I had the honour of giving the Barlow Dante Lectures in University College, London. The great pleasure I felt at this invitation, and at the welcome extended by Professor Laura Lepschy and her colleagues, was enhanced by the suggestion that the lectures be published under the auspices of the Society for Italian Studies.

In the pages that follow I have tried to retain the less formal aspects of my spoken text as far as possible; a few passages have been expanded, and documentation — necessarily on a modest scale — has been added.

The three essays, like the lectures on which they are based, are far-reachingly interrelated, yet they remain three individual, and deliberately selective, contributions. To attempt anything more comprehensive in brief compass, such as offering a complete reading of Dante's *Convivio*, would merely be an act of foolish hubris. The discussions focus on only a few of the key problems in and around the *Convivio*; the approaches to these are diverse but I hope complementary. The main concerns of the three essays are: the nature of the bonds between *Vita Nuova* and *Convivio*; the nature and significance of the Donna Gentile, Dante's 'second love'; and the imaginative and intellectual coherence of the third and fourth treatises of the *Convivio*, which are so often viewed as divergent and as separated by a deep caesura or crisis in Dante's thought.

Choosing these as my focal questions clearly meant that much else had to be excluded. There is little here, for instance, on the relations between Dante's *Convivio* and his *Monarchia*; there is almost nothing on the controversial issue of how far there is harmony or disharmony between the *Convivio* and the *Commedia*. Only a brief excursus added at the close comments on the Donna Gentile's subsequent fate — but at the hands of scholars, rather than at Dante's own.

The subtitle of this monograph, 'The Originality and the Contexts of the *Convivio*', is probably too large and too ambitious for what is offered, but at least it will serve to indicate the areas where I have attempted some new detailed explorations. The literary context which is meant is primarily that of the *Vita Nuova* and a few of the *Rime*; the intellectual context is, first, one that can in broadest terms be called the Neoplatonic: especially the *Liber de causis*, the Hermetic treatise *Asclepius*, and Boethius' *Consolation of Philosophy*; and second, the Aristotelian, with particular reference to Albert's and Thomas's commentaries on the *Ethics* and to two brief, keenly individual treatises by the Averroist Boethius of Dacia. The more specifically historical and political context of the fourth treatise of the *Convivio* falls outside my scope; it has been illuminated outstandingly in recent times in a group of studies by Charles T.

Davis, now united in his volume *Dante's Italy and Other Essays* (Philadelphia, 1984).

It is a marvellous moment at which to try to set down some thoughts about the *Convivio*: one can enter a dialogue which for several decades has stimulated the highest levels of scholarship and interpretation. After Bruno Nardi had, over half a century, elucidated the main intellectual difficulties, and had penetrated Dante's philosophical reading more profoundly than anyone before him, 1988 saw the publication of Cesare Vasoli's admirable commentary on the prose of the *Convivio*, integrating much of Nardi's work and juxtaposing it with his own perceptions and those of other scholars, with a finesse of judgement that few exegetes can equal. His work is complemented by Domenico De Robertis's sensitive poetic commentaries on the canzoni in the *Convivio* volume, as well as by the new, long-awaited critical text of the *Convivio* by Franca Brambilla Ageno (1995). For the other texts that enter my argument, one need only mention De Robertis's edition of the *Vita Nuova*, Gianfranco Contini's of the *Rime*, and, last not least, the superbly detailed commentary of Kenelm Foster and Patrick Boyde in their edition of *Dante's Lyric Poetry*[1] to see how privileged any scholar is who at this point attempts a fresh consideration of aspects of these writings, which have already attracted so many insights of such rare quality.

Kernilien, August 1996 — Peter Dronke

[1] Full references to the editions mentioned in this paragraph are given in Ch. I n. 1.

I

FROM BEATRICE TO THE DONNA GENTILE

What is the relation between Dante's first and his second love — between Beatrice, the heroine of his *Vita Nuova*, and the Donna Gentile, the heroine of his *Convivio*? We who know the *Commedia* know that Dante's first love, Beatrice, was also his last — the heavenly guide whom he rediscovers in his otherworld. But that rediscovery falls outside the scope of the present study, in which I shall glance only rarely at works later than the *Convivio* itself. For the earlier group of writings, the first problem — inescapably — is what appears to be a series of contradictions between the *Vita Nuova*, the work composed around 1292-93, which is the summation of the poetry and strivings of Dante's youth, and the *Convivio*, composed between 1304 and 1307, the first major work of his maturity.[1]

The problem, in briefest, simplifying terms, is this. The Donna Gentile first enters as a character near the close of the *Vita Nuova*: she is the compassionate lady who consoles Dante, still desperate with grief more than a year after Beatrice's death, and who gradually inspires new feelings of love in him. In the *Vita Nuova* Dante goes on to berate himself for those feelings and, through the force of Beatrice's image, to overcome them: at the close of the work he is granted a vision of his first love in heavenly glory, and resolves to write of her again, to tell of her what has never yet been told of any woman.

Twelve years or so later, Dante in the *Convivio* refers several times to the *Vita Nuova*, and makes all this sound as if it had happened quite differently. He is composing for a readership whom he assumes to be familiar with his earlier work. Near the opening of the *Convivio*, he says he does not intend to detract from the *Vita Nuova* in any way: if it was composed in a fervid and passionate style, whilst his *Convivio* will be temperate and mature, this is only reasonable, since they belong to different ages of his life.[2] But lest anyone think that after Beatrice's

[1] In what follows, the *Vita Nuova* (*VN*) is cited from the ed. of Domenico De Robertis (Milan-Naples, 1980), repr. in Dante Alighieri, *Opere minori* I/1, Milan-Naples, 1984). The *Convivio* is cited, except when otherwise noted, from the ed. of Cesare Vasoli and Domenico De Robertis, *Opere minori* I/2 (Milan-Naples, 1988). References to the text are prefaced by '*Conv.*', and to the commentary by 'Vasoli'. The new critical ed. of the *Convivio* by Franca Brambilla Ageno (3 vols., Florence, 1995), cited as 'Ageno', has also been consulted throughout. Dante's *Rime* are cited from the ed. of Kenelm Foster and Patrick Boyde, *Dante's Lyric Poetry, I The Poems: Text and Translation, II Commentary* (Oxford, 1967), cited as 'Foster-Boyde'; the ed. of the *Rime* by Gianfranco Contini in *Opere minori* I/1, and that of the *Rime della maturità e dell'esilio* by Michele Barbi and Vincenzo Pernicone (Florence, 1969), have likewise been consulted for many passages. English translations of texts cited are my own throughout (though naturally I have often looked across the page at the Foster-Boyde translations of the *Rime*, and have assuredly profited from this).

[2] *Conv.* I, i, 16.

death he found consolation in an unworthy love, Dante explains that the gentle lady who comforted him was an allegorical figure: she was Philosophy, who consoled him as she had once consoled the grieving Boethius in his prison. So now, referring to those same episodes in the *Vita Nuova*, Dante claims that they depicted the desire for his second beloved not at all as being condemned or overcome, but as growing and at last gaining the ascendancy, until for the sake of the Donna Gentile, Philosophy, he set aside the memory of his first love.

By his repeated allusions to the *Vita Nuova* in his new work, Dante almost defiantly forces his more attentive readers to note these contradictions. And he has been blessed with many attentive readers, especially in our century. To cope with the anomalies, they have come up with every possible kind of solution — and some impossible ones as well. Some of the principal moves have been these: The Donna Gentile, when she makes her first appearance in the *Vita Nuova*, is a real woman, who, by way of her compassion for Dante, becomes a real erotic temptation; Dante, still ashamed of this at the time of writing the *Convivio*, goes to great lengths to pretend that she never really existed and that his only consolation after Beatrice's death was Philosophy. Or again, it is argued that in the earlier as well as in the later work the Donna Gentile is purely an allegory, or purely a symbol, and that the language of temptation, baseness and shame in the earlier one is merely an elaborate fiction, merely an instance of the 'fervid and passionate' way of expression characteristic of the youthful work. Sometimes this view is enriched by the claim that Beatrice, like the Donna Gentile, is purely an allegory, or purely a symbol, too — that the whole of the *Vita Nuova* should, like the *Convivio*, be read allegorically. I shall return to this approach later — though I should like to say at once that the habitual use by many Dante scholars of 'allegory' and 'symbol' as if they were synonyms seems to me an anachronism and a serious error in method: the terms *allegoria* and *symbolum* reflect two wholly distinct traditions in the Latin Middle Ages,[3] and in the years around 1300 could not possibly have carried the same meaning or connotations.

But granting that the Donna Gentile was from the outset allegorical (or for that matter symbolic) doesn't help to resolve the further problem: why is she presented as vanquished by the all-conquering memory of Beatrice towards the end of the *Vita Nuova*, if the *Convivio* affirms that the *Vita Nuova* near its close shows the Donna Gentile victorious? It is this that led to the view — most trenchantly expounded by Bruno Nardi — that the *Vita Nuova*, at the time Dante wrote the *Convivio*, had a different close from the one we know: an ending showing in detail how the Donna Gentile eclipsed Beatrice, an ending that today is lost. What survives, on this account, is only a *Vita Nuova* that was revised after

[3] Cf. my study *Fabula: Explorations into the Uses of Myth in Medieval Platonism* (Leiden-Cologne, 1974); for the principal relevant passages, see the Index, s.v. *allegoria*, allegory (p. 196) and s.v. symbol, *symbolum* (p. 200).

Dante broke off the *Convivio* — revised specifically with a view to preparing the glorious reappearance of Beatrice in the *Commedia*.[4]

Some cogent objections have also been made to this hypothesis, first by André Pézard, then, more fully, in an essay by Mario Marti, with the delightful title 'Life and death of the presumed double redaction of the *Vita Nuova*' (1965). It was generally accepted, for some years at least, that Marti had dealt the hypothetical earlier, pro-Donna-Gentile version of the *Vita Nuova* its death-blow — yet in 1983 this version re-emerged from its tomb, peering around more cautiously than before, in some thoughtful pages in Maria Corti's *La felicità mentale*.[5]

Yet another series of moves is made by the many scholars who try to minimize the contradictions between *Vita Nuova* and *Convivio*, or to show that these are only apparent and not real. A notable older — though in some aspects eccentric — attempt at harmonizing the two works was that of Étienne Gilson, in his *Dante et la Philosophie* (1939).[6] Since then, many subtle and textually acute observations that go in the direction of harmonizing have been made particularly by some of Dante's editors: Foster-Boyde and Contini for the *Rime*, De Robertis for the *Vita Nuova*, Vasoli with De Robertis for the *Convivio*. None, however, has gone so far as to claim that all the contradictions can be neatly resolved.

Any serious discussion of the *Convivio*, and in particular of the rôle of the Donna Gentile, must try to take account of the major scholarly contributions of recent decades, divergent as these are, and at the same time must face the problems afresh. Can one hope to make some headway, to see something illuminating that has not emerged clearly hitherto? My own difficulty is partly that I can see the force of even the most diametrically opposed arguments: it seems to me, for instance, that several of Nardi's insights were — and remain — penetrating, and that Marti, refuting Nardi, was equally penetrating. So in what follows I shall attempt a fresh *lectura* of some of the principal passages relevant

4 'S'ha da credere a Dante o ai suoi critici?', *Cultura Neolatina*, 2 (1942), 327-33 (= 'Dalla prima alla seconda "Vita Nuova"', in his *Nel mondo di Dante*, Rome, 1944, pp. 3-20).

5 André Pézard, 'Avatars de la Donna gentile' (1949), repr. as 'Dante et quelques dames gentilles' in his *Dans le sillage de Dante* (Paris, 1975), pp. 27-36; Mario Marti, 'Vita e morte della presunta doppia redazione della *Vita Nuova*', *Rivista di cultura classica e medievale*, 7 (1965), [= *Studi in onore di Alfredo Schiaffini*], 657-69; Maria Corti, *La felicità mentale. Nuove prospettive per Cavalcanti e Dante* (Turin, 1983), pp. 146-55.

6 I cite the English translation: *Dante the Philosopher* (London, 1948). Quite apart from the repeated insistence that the Donna Gentile is 'only a symbol' (p. 88), 'only the symbol of philosophy' (p. 90), Gilson has a simplistic argument presenting Beatrice as the presiding genius of the *Convivio*: 'Dante speaks [in the *Convivio*] as a man who has already been won back by the heavenly Beatrice' (p. 93); 'the whole narrative of the Second Treatise . . . has the immediate object of placing the entire work under the patronage of Beatrice' (p. 100). Notwithstanding certain phrases, discussed below, that seem to point in this direction, it is hard to accept a reading of *Convivio* II that so blandly glosses over the question of conflict between Dante's two 'thoughts'. This seems to me one of the weak points in a book which also contains many insights that remain unsurpassed (see especially Bruno Nardi's long review article in *Nel mondo di Dante*, cit. n. 4, pp. 209-45).

to the problems, in the *Vita Nuova* and *Convivio* and also in the *Rime*, but alluding to the disparate views of scholars only eclectically, sometimes in order to highlight certain points, and just now and then to register a disagreement.

The rôle of allegory in the *Convivio* is evident, at least in treatises II and III, where Dante gives a meticulous allegorical as well as literal reading of two of his canzoni. If he had completed the other eleven treatises he'd planned, other canzoni too would doubtless have been given their allegorêsis. The part that allegory plays in the *Vita Nuova* is less systematic and somewhat elusive to define. There is clearly quite a lot of what today is often called personification-allegory. Amore is personified throughout, as Dante himself explains in detail (*VN* XXV); Amore often speaks, as do for instance the spirits within Dante — the vital, animal, and natural — who are personified at the opening of the work (*VN* II, 4-7); Death is personified in many passages, verse and prose, from Dante's lyrical invective *Morte villana* (*VN* VIII, 8-11) onwards; the Ballata that Dante sends to Beatrice (*VN* XII, 10-15) is spoken to as if it were a human messenger; or again, in the sonnet *Tutti li miei penser*, Lady Compassion, *madonna la Pietà*, is invoked both as enemy and as protectress (*VN* XIII, 8-9).[7] On the other hand, such a moment as the 'wondrous vision' of Amore compelling Beatrice to eat Dante's heart (*VN* III) is not an allegory, at least in the standard sense that the Middle Ages inherited from Quintilian, of 'showing one thing by the words, another (even at times the contrary) by the meaning'.[8] For here the meaning is scarcely detachable from the vision itself. This vision could sooner be called an enigma, in the sense defined by Isidore of Seville, who (unusually in the Latin tradition) sharply demarcates enigma from allegory: he affirms that an enigma is 'an obscure meaning alone, adumbrated by means of certain images';[9] and it is a single, obscure visionary scene, with no clearly corresponding veiled meaning, which Dante here sets as a challenge to his poet-friends to interpret.

Where, then, in the *Vita Nuova* do we get an instance of an allegorical correspondence in precisely Quintilian's sense? The nearest, perhaps, is in Chapter XXIX, where Dante demonstrates that the number nine was Beatrice herself. Here the words show one thing — the number nine — and they signify another: Beatrice. The reason this number was constantly associated with Beatrice (was her 'friend' — *amico* — as Dante puts it three times), was 'to signify that she was a nine, that is, a miracle, whose root is solely the miraculous Trinity'. Yet even here the term *allegoria* does not occur: Dante says instead that the nine signifies Beatrice *per similitudine* (XXIX, 3), by way of a likeness or similitude.

The term *simbolo*, which Dante does not use in the *Vita Nuova* or for that matter in the *Convivio*, has as its root concept neither personification nor vision

[7] Dante discusses the rhetorical figure prosopopeia, 'quando a le cose inanimate si parla', at *Conv.* III, ix, 2.

[8] *Institutio Oratoria*, VIII, 6, 44.

[9] *Etymologiae*, I, 37, 26.

(whether clear or enigmatic), nor allegory in the traditional sense, by which words say one thing and mean another: the root concept lies rather in the showing of what cannot be seen or put into words. The whole of the Christian Neoplatonic tradition, from pseudo-Dionysius and in particular his translator Eriugena, through whom the word *symbolum* becomes acclimatized in the Latin West, emphasizes the elusive, unfathomable aspect of symbolism.[10] In Richard of St Victor's definition,[11] *Symbolum est collectio formarum visibilium ad invisibilium demonstrationem* — a symbol is a gathering of visible forms for the showing of the invisible. We can, if we wish, understand *formarum* a second time — i.e. for the showing of invisible *forms* — yet this is not necessary: the *invisibilia* that are shown when a symbolist gathers visible forms can comprise whatever pertains to the invisible realm. In what follows, to leave this flexible, I shall retain the term *invisibilia*.

The reason Dante does not allude to the Christian Neoplatonic concept *symbolum*, as he will have found it especially in Richard of St Victor, is not, I suggest, because it lay outside his interests. Rather, because to him as a poet the gathering of visible forms for the showing of *invisibilia* was second nature: it was something he did so spontaneously and often that he did not see it as requiring commentary. From the outset of the *Vita Nuova* it is natural for the *visibilia* of the narrative to be charged with meaning that reaches beyond themselves. Thus the visible Beatrice's greeting (*salute*) shows the *invisibile* of Dante's salvation: 'in it dwelt all my beatitude'; the apparition of the visible Beatrice shows the invisible inner reality: 'a flame of charity arose in me which made me pardon whoever had offended me'.[12] The way in which Amore features as a poetic personification, or the way in which the number nine 'is the friend of' Beatrice — these are things such as Dante believed needed some exegesis. But the ways in which the visible Florentine girl reveals *invisibilia* are made evident at every stage of the narrative. They need no analysis: they define themselves, we could say, in a series of ostensive definitions, and are consubstantial with Dante's poetic art.

What I should like to suggest is, first, that symbolism, for Dante as for the entire Christian Neoplatonic tradition, is based in visible forms and is elaborated by way of visible forms. Second, that in the *Vita Nuova* Dante presents both Beatrice and the Donna Gentile as visible forms. This suggestion is here made quite independently of any biographical speculations scholars may engage in — such as whether it is historically true that both young women actually lived in Florence when Dante was young. What matters poetically is that both Beatrice

[10] Cf. *Fabula* (cit. n. 3), esp. pp. 44-46.

[11] *In Apocalypsim*, I, 1 (P. L. 196, 686 f.). A similar formulation, which may well be slightly older, is found in Hugh of St Victor, *Expositiones in Hierarchiam caelestem*, 3 (P. L. 175, 960). Nonetheless, my primary reference here is to Richard, because of Dante's known admiration for him. There are, I believe, good reasons for conjecturing that Dante read the Apocalypse with the help of Richard's commentary: see my 'L'Apocalisse negli ultimi canti del *Purgatorio*', in *Dante e la Bibbia*, ed. Giovanni Barblan (Florence, 1988), pp. 81-94.

[12] *VN* X, 3; XI, 1.

and the Donna Gentile are imagined and brought on as living women. Third, I would argue that not only Beatrice but also the Donna Gentile is a visible form showing *invisibilia.* That is, I would reject the alternatives so often put forward by scholars, that the Donna Gentile is either 'merely an erotic experience' or 'merely a symbol'. The second alternative usually turns out to be a confused way of saying 'she is from the start an allegory or personification of Philosophy, who never had any human reality, living or imagined'. It is confused in that it takes no account of the accepted meaning of *symbolum* up to and in Dante's time. But it also seems to me untrue to Dante's text — just as untrue as the claim that he was describing something 'merely erotic'.

Let us look more closely at some features of the last part of the *Vita Nuova* with these suggestions in mind.

The initial mention of Dante's second love comes in *Vita Nuova* XXXV. The time is more than a year after Beatrice's death. This death, Dante tells, still causes in him such marks of suffering that, embarrassed, he lifts his eyes to see if anyone could be watching him in such a state. A gentle lady (*gentile donna* — a phrase that had already been used three times of Beatrice herself) was looking from a window, so compassionately that the whole of compassion seemed to be gathered in her. Dante, as he withdraws, so that she shall not see his tears and the full extent of his wretchedness, is sure that her compassion must be accompanied by most noble love (*nobilissimo amore*), and in the sonnet that follows he reflects:

> Ben è con quella donna quello Amore
> lo qual mi face andar così piangendo.
>
> Indeed with that lady is the same Amore
> who makes me go about weeping thus.

The lady's face, the prose continues (*VN* XXXVI), which was pale as if with love, had a colouring that reminded Dante of the colour of Beatrice's face. So far, then, the text reveals a second visible form, visible in precisely the same way as Beatrice had been — a form, that is, of the same order of imaginative reality as she. And she likewise from the outset shows *invisibilia*: she shows — Dante conceives — the totality of compassion, and a love inseparable from that compassion and from Dante's own grieving.

Then some complications arise. Earlier (XXXI, 1), when Dante's eyes were so weary with weeping for Beatrice 'that they could not give vent to my sadness (*non poteano disfogare la mia tristizia*), I thought of trying to give vent to it with some dolorous words': this impulse had brought forth the canzone *Li occhi dolenti.* Now, with deceptively similar phrasing, Dante says something rather different: 'And certainly many times, unable to weep or to give vent to my sadness (*disfogare la mia tristizia*), I went to see this compassionate lady, who looked as if she might draw forth the tears from my eyes through the sight of her' (XXXVI, 2).

Here, that is, it is no longer that Dante has wept his fill, but that he needs the new incentive in order to weep for Beatrice yet again. And yet the sonnet that follows becomes more of a *lode* of the living lady's compassion, and ends with the admission that, while his eyes still long to weep,

> . . . voi crescete sì lor volontate,
> che de la voglia si consuman tutti;
> ma lagrimar dinanzi a voi non sanno.

> . . . you so increase their longing
> that by the wanting they are all consumed;
> but in your presence they don't know how to weep.

By way of a telling verbal ambiguity, Dante shows his grieving intention transforming itself into sensual desire. *Volontate* and *voglia* mean both the will and desire to weep Beatrice, while gazing at the Donna Gentile, and the nascent new will and desire for her. The *ma* that opens the last line of the sonnet is the first indication that this new desire is about to gain ascendancy, and that a new *invisibile* will be shown.

This introduces the psychomachia in which Dante's eyes 'began to delight too much in seeing her', and the poet reviles himself and curses his eyes for their lack of steadfastness. He claims to be sure that the Donna Gentile gazes at him only out of sorrow for the glorious lady whom he has lost. The sonnet that follows (XXXVII, 6-8) again adds a thought of which there is no hint in the prose: Dante, accusing his eyes, exclaims: 'Your fickleness afflicts and terrifies me, so that I greatly fear (*ch'io temo forte*) the face of a lady who gazes at you'. Once more the phrasing recalls an earlier expression: in the previous sonnet (XXXVI, 4) Dante had said 'that I greatly fear (*ch'io temo forte*) my heart may break' — and there the cause was still the memory of Beatrice. Now the fear is inspired by the Donna Gentile's gaze. It is a fear compounded of two elements: Dante is afraid of being drawn to her even more the more their eyes meet, and afraid that she will see through to his disloyalty, to the changed look in his eyes.

In the next section (*VN* XXXVIII), the psychomachia is both dilated and intensified. Dante was many times thinking of the Donna Gentile 'as of a person who pleased me too much'; he sees her not only as young and beautiful but as wise (*savia*); 'perhaps she has appeared through Amore's will, so that my life may know peace. And many times I thought of her more amorously, until my heart consented to this, that is, to its loving thought'. This last phrase is echoed significantly in the *Convivio*, with explicit reference to this passage: 'And as is told by me in that little book, more because of her gentleness than of my own choice it came about that I consented to be hers'.[13] Yet here, in the *Vita Nuova* itself, the thoughts continue to do battle, the one recoiling in horror at the baseness of such consolation (*in così vile modo*), the other offering release, through a lady who is both noble and full of pity. If the thought of her was noble (*gentile*) on account of its object, in other respects, says Dante, it was 'most base' (*vilissimo*, XXXVIII, 4). This is one of several such vehement expressions that present something of a stumbling-block to any naïve acceptance of the *Convivio*'s reinterpretation of these moments: to have felt desire for the consolation of Philosophy more than a year after Beatrice's death might — given all Dante's claims for the sublimity of his first love — conceivably be called inopportune; but *vilissimo*? As a poetic fiction it is, to say the least, extravagant.

In the prose, the clash of the conflicting thoughts has a montage that I would see as very close to that of the climactic scene in Augustine's *Confessions*, the inner struggle which leads directly to his moment of conversion.[14] In the sonnet that follows (XXXVIII, 8-10), Dante has another literary model in view: it is a debate between body and soul, or eye and heart, or sensuality and reason — a genre that had reached poetic heights in Latin in the twelfth and early thirteenth centuries, with Peter of Blois and Philip the Chancellor.[15] The heart, which Dante in the prose has identified with *appetito* (sensual appetite), disputes with the soul about the gentle thought of consenting to love the consoler, the new beloved. Two points have not been remarked even in the three admirable modern commentaries known to me. In the verses

> L'anima dice al cor: 'Chi è costui,
> che vene a consolar la nostra mente . . .?'
>
> The soul says to the heart: 'Who is this one
> who comes to console our mind . . .?'

the masculine form *costui*, referring to the thought (*penser*) of the Donna Gentile, has perhaps masked the echo which I believe Dante intends: one that had passed from the Song of Songs — *Quae est ista quae ascendit* . . . — into Cavalcanti's sonnet, *Chi è questa che vèn* . . .[16] Cavalcanti, like Dante, was consciously playing upon the connotations of the Solomonic beloved, seen equally as the Bride in the Canticle and the womanly figure of Wisdom in the 'Sapiential'

[13] Compare *VN* XXXVIII, 1: 'E molte volte pensava più amorosamente, tanto che lo cuore consentiva in lui, cioè nel suo ragionare', and *Conv.* II, ii, 2: 'E sì come è ragionato per me ne lo allegato libello, più da sua gentilezza che da mia elezione venne ch'io ad essere suo consentisse'.

[14] Cf. *Conf.* VIII, 11, 25 ff.

[15] On Peter of Blois's debates, see 'Peter of Blois and Poetry at the Court of Henry II', in my *The Medieval Poet and his World* (Rome, 1984), esp. pp. 291-314. The two most notable 'psychological' altercations by Philip the Chancellor are *Quisquis cordis et oculi* (*Analecta Hymnica*, 21, 114 f.) and *Inter membra singula* (ibid. 116 f.).

[16] On the variant versions of this phrase (Cant. 6, 9 and 8, 5) and their influence, cf. 'The Song of Songs and Medieval Love-Lyric', in *The Medieval Poet* (cit. n. 15), pp. 209-36, at pp. 211 f.

books. The *invisibilia* which the visible form of the Donna Gentile shows are increasing: the totality of compassion, the love inseparable from that compassion, and — in at least certain poetic hints — the wisdom inseparable from both: she is *savia*, and the thought of her advent is introduced with words that cannot but suggest the advent of Sapientia.

The other point I would stress is the paradox: it is the sensual heart which answers the soul's question and affirms the origin of the loving thought in the compassionate lady. Sensuality here guides reason towards the fuller recognition of that lady who in the *Convivio* will be revealed as reason's supreme embodiment.

The last four sections of the *Vita Nuova* comprehend what can only be called a wholehearted reaffirmation of Beatrice and a contrite rejection of the loving desire for the Donna Gentile. It is this second aspect on which we must focus here.

A vision of Beatrice as a young child, in the crimson dress in which Dante had first beheld her, now causes his heart 'dolorously to repent of the desire by which it had let itself be so basely possessed for some days, against the constancy of reason' (XXXIX, 2). Dante insists it was a wicked desire (*malvagio desiderio*), and that his thoughts then returned to Beatrice 'with all my shame-filled heart' (*con tutto lo vergognoso cuore*). The remorseful sonnet he then composes is meant to show the audience and readers of the previous sonnets, which had welcomed the Donna Gentile, that the 'wicked desire and vain temptation' (XXXIX, 6) had been destroyed beyond all doubt. Two further sonnets — poetically the crowning ones of the *Vita Nuova* — celebrate Beatrice lost, and Beatrice among the saints in the empyrean. The first is the imagined address to the pilgrims passing through Florence (XL, 9-10):

> Oh you pilgrims who go lost in thought,
> perhaps of something that is far from you,
> do you come from such a distant land
> (for that is what your aspect indicates)
> as not to weep when you pass
> through the midst of the sorrowing city?[17]

[17] *VN* XL, 9-10:

> Deh peregrini che pensosi andate,
> forse di cosa che non v'è presente,
> venite voi da sì lontana gente,
> com'a la vista voi ne dimostrate,
> che non piangete quando voi passate
> per lo suo mezzo la città dolente . . .?

Both Foster-Boyde (II, 154) and De Robertis (p. 240) note Dante's subtle adaptation here of Luke 24, 18. One should perhaps add that, in the twelfth and thirteenth centuries, the words from Luke had become the kernel of the medieval Latin *Peregrinus* plays (cf. Karl Young, *The Drama of the Medieval Church*, 2 vols., Oxford, 1933, esp. I, 451-83).

The city is bereft of its beatifier, its *beatrice*. This is followed, in the sonnet *Oltre la spera*, by Dante's 'peregrine spirit' making its pilgrimage beyond the highest of the circling spheres, to bring back to the dazed poet the blissful name which remains as his vestige of understanding of the heavenly world (XLI, 10-13). This leads to the final vision, never disclosed, 'in which I saw things that made me resolve to say no more about this blessed one till I could treat of her more fittingly. And to arrive at that point I strive as much as I can, as she truly knows. So that, if it please him for whom all things live that my life should continue for some years, I hope to tell of her what was never yet told of any woman' (XLII, 1-2).

Without a word the Donna Gentile has left the scene — reduced to a wicked desire that's been repented of. Dante's final resolution proposes a future atonement in his writing. In my view, it is perfectly possible to imagine Dante setting down these words of resolve around 1293, as he was concluding the extant *Vita Nuova*. They need not, *pace* Nardi, have been added to the work at a far later date, when Dante already had his *Commedia* planned. And they cannot, *pace* Foster-Boyde, refer to the *Vita Nuova* itself:[18] for Dante, as he brings this work to its close, hopes precisely for the added life to compose a greater work for Beatrice, now that this one is done. Nor again, *pace* Maria Corti,[19] is there anything strange about a man as young as twenty-eight (as Dante would have been at the time) praying to be granted life enough to achieve his purpose — not strange, at least, in a world as dangerous as that of Florentine politics at that moment. Dante's expression does not of itself suggest to me a later point in time.

We shall see that some of Dante's *Rime*, as well as the *Convivio*, take up again the conflict between his first and his second love. Yet what Dante says at the close of the *Vita Nuova* may help to set that conflict in perspective. Notwithstanding all the vividness of its depiction, in the *Vita Nuova* and later, the repeated changes of stance, the battles of opposing *pensieri* and *spiriti*, the retractions and palinodes, Dante's psychomachia in the last resort resolves itself in poetic play — even if it is the play of an unusually intense imagination. And still, behind all the play — this seems to be the import of the last section of the youthful work — there is a unique early experience which to Dante is so ineradicable that he affirms his intent to revert to it more splendidly (even if in 1293 he had little idea of the form this reversion might take).

Meanwhile the imagined conflict between the first and second loves is projected in other modes. In the elaborately wrought canzone, *Voi che 'ntendendo il terzo ciel movete*, that opens the second treatise of the *Convivio*, but that was probably composed soon after the completion of the *Vita Nuova*,[20] the *symbola*

[18] *Dante's Lyric Poetry*, II, 155: 'The *Vita Nuova* is in itself "quello che mai non fue detto d'alcuna" — praise such as had never before been accorded to a woman'.

[19] *La felicità mentale* (cit. n. 5), p. 153.

[20] Foster-Boyde no. 59; on the date of composition, and the difficulties raised by this canzone, see especially their Appendix, 'The Biographical Problems in "Voi che 'ntendendo"', II, 341-62.

latent in the language of the earlier sonnets are exchanged for a consciously sustained allegory, in which a second meaning distinct from the literal can be traced — as Dante in his prose exposition traces it — matching the literal point by point. That this second meaning was present, though veiled, in the canzone from the outset, and not superadded later, is strongly hinted by Dante in his *congedo*: 'My song, I think they will be rare who understand your meaning well — so demanding and difficult is the way that you express it . . .'.

Dante invokes the Intelligences, or angels, of the heaven of Venus, to tell them of his new condition — the new spirit of love contending with the old. For Dante, as for most medieval intellectuals, the Intelligences were no mere figures of speech: they influence the volitions and actions of human beings, even if (in the view of all but the most radical astrologers) they don't completely determine these. While the thought of Beatrice in glory sustained Dante in his sorrow after she had died, the thought of another lady, the Donna Gentile, now displaces it and dominates Dante, affirming that salvation lies in gazing into her eyes (*Chi veder vol la salute,* | *faccia che li occhi d'esta donna miri*).

The consoling thought that was Beatrice grows fainter[21] and can only cry out at its own defeat, or death. The new thought counters: what seems to you to be death is merely confusion and fear: don't be afraid, give your allegiance wholly now to the new lady, who is so compassionate and benign (*umile*); submit to your lord, Amor.

Perhaps these few brief allusions to the movement of thought in the canzone will help sharpen the focus on the contradictions with the *Vita Nuova* that emerge in both the literal explanation and the allegorêsis that follow.

Dante affirms that, because 'that gentle lady whom I mentioned at the close of the *Vita Nuova* . . . showed herself impassioned by such great mercy on account of my widowed life', he consented to be hers. But now the terms of the conflict with the memory of Beatrice have profoundly changed. His new love 'needs some time and nurturing of thoughts' in order to become great and perfect — before that, there is 'many a battle' between the thoughts of the first and the second love.[22] Yet as the second was aided continually by seeing the Donna Gentile, it increased, which the thought of Beatrice, looking back into the past, could not: so when Dante began the canzone *Voi che 'ntendendo,* he says 'I directed my voice to the region from which the *victory* of the new thought came, which was *most virtuous,* like a celestial power'.[23]

The expression 'most virtuous' (*virtuosissimo*), coming so soon after Dante's explicit reference to his *Vita Nuova,* cannot but recall to the readers of that work the expression 'most base' (*vilissimo*), which Dante had there used of that same thought. And there there had been no question of any victory of the new — only

[21] As Dante explains (*Conv.* II, vi, 7), while the memory was stronger, he called this thought his *anima,* the other, *spirito.*

[22] *Conv.* II, ii, 1-3.

[23] *Conv.* II, ii, 5 (italics mine).

of repentance and atonement for a brief 'wicked desire' for a second love. Shall we say then, with Nardi, that originally the *Vita Nuova* too must have ended with the victory and praise of the second thought and the second love? Insofar as the *Convivio* words which herald this victory — 'as is told by me in that little book' — suggest Dante is summarizing the close of the *Vita Nuova*, that would indeed be the implication. Or should we agree with Marti and Pézard that this is an unsatisfactory hypothesis, which, even if it were accepted, would not do away with the difficulties it is designed to meet? Quite apart from the fact that there is not a trace of such an earlier *Vita Nuova* in the manuscript tradition, if Dante, preparing the *Commedia*, became dissatisfied with that earlier version, which ended — as the *Convivio* appears to suggest — with the Donna Gentile's ascendancy over Beatrice, why in his revision did Dante still leave glaring discrepancies between the two works? Or again, if at this later point in his life and work Dante had become unhappy about the montage of the *Convivio*, and thought solely of glorifying Beatrice, could he not perfectly well have destroyed the *Convivio* and made it disappear as completely as that hypothetical first *Vita Nuova*?

But Marti's most stringent point was this. We have external evidence, through some sonnets that Cecco Angiolieri addressed to Dante, that the sonnet *Oltre la spera*, which celebrates Beatrice in the empyrean, with Dante's loving thought mounting to her there, was composed and known already before 1303. That is, this glorification of Beatrice, this magnificently decisive climax of the *Vita Nuova*, predates the *Convivio*. The victory of Beatrice in the *Vita Nuova*, that is, cannot have been due to a later, post-*Convivio* revision.[24]

In some way, then, we must embrace the contradictions between the two works; what counts is rather to see more precisely how we should do so, and in particular, in what ways Dante stimulates us to doing so. Thus for instance, even within what the *Convivio* says about Beatrice there are some arresting anomalies. In the very chapter in which the literal explanation of *Voi che 'ntendendo* begins, she is evoked in the present tense as well as in the past: she is 'that blessed Beatrice who lives (*che vive*) in heaven with the angels and on earth with my soul' — even though the thought of her, 'which was still holding (*tenea ancora*) the fortress of my mind for that glorious Beatrice',[25] was about to be defeated by the thought of the Donna Gentile. And what are we to make of Beatrice's final appearance in the *Convivio*, six chapters later? Dante there affirms that a discussion of the immortality of the soul, to which he then proceeds, 'will be a beautiful way of concluding my speaking of that living blessed Beatrice, of

[24] On Nardi's attempt to postulate a further original Donna Gentile episode after *Oltre la spera*, and to make a sharp distinction between the consoling lady of the *Vita Nuova* and the Donna Gentile of the *Convivio*, in an essay 'Dante e Guido Cavalcanti', *Giornale storico della letteratura italiana*, 139 (1962), 481-512, see Marti's conclusive objections, art. cit. (n. 5), pp. 666-69.

[25] *Conv.* II, ii, 1 and 3.

whom, by my resolve, I do not intend to say more in this book'.[26] After offering a range of arguments — drawing on rhetoric and theology as well as philosophy — for a life after death, Dante concludes the chapter: 'And so I believe, so I affirm, and so I am certain of passing to another, better life after this one, where that glorious lady lives of whom my soul was enamoured when it was contending'[27] — in strife with its own feelings about the thought of the second love.

The resolve to say no more about Beatrice in the *Convivio* manifestly echoes the resolve at the close of the *Vita Nuova*, 'to say no more of this blessed one till I can treat of her more fittingly', and indicates to those who also know the earlier work that this time is not yet at hand. And Dante's passionate expression, in the *Convivio* itself, of the conviction that he too will find his place in heaven, 'where that glorious lady lives' — if anything could be called an early augury of the *Commedia*, surely it would be this. Dante's bold paradox is to place it here strategically, at the very moment when the ascendancy of the Donna Gentile is about to be described.

When Dante turns (II, xii) to the 'allegorical and true' exposition of *Voi che 'ntendendo*, the solace that he found 'after some time' (*dopo alquanto tempo*), when at first he had been inconsolable at Beatrice's death, came to him from reading Boethius' *Consolation of Philosophy* and Cicero's book *On Friendship* (in which the consolation for the loss of a dear friend is bound up with arguments for an immortal life after death). Dante then recognizes that Philosophy was the *donna* of Boethius and Cicero (the two authors whom he later allegorizes as Intelligences of the heaven of Venus, which has itself allegorically become the sphere of Rhetoric). He fully convinces himself that the Philosophia known to Boethius and Cicero was the highest of beings, and says 'I imagined her fashioned like a noble lady, and I could not imagine her in any attitude except a merciful one'. Unable to turn from gazing at her, he followed her to the places where she showed herself — the schools of the religious and the disputations of the philosophers. In a short time, perhaps thirty months, Dante adds, he began to have so great a sense of her sweetness that love of her chased out and destroyed every other thought, even that of his first love. It was this inner condition that he showed 'under the figure of other things' (*sotto figura d'altre cose*) in his canzone: for no vernacular was yet equipped to celebrate Philosophy direct in poetry, nor was there yet an audience who could readily have understood such a celebration. Last not least, Dante's first audience, he claims, would have believed him capable of a new human love, but not of a love of Philosophy, 'the daughter of God, queen of all, noblest and most beautiful'.

I should like to suggest that we look more closely at the implications of that expression *sotto figura d'altre cose*. It was Auerbach's merit to perceive that,

[26] *Conv.* II, viii, 7.

[27] Ibid. 16: 'e io così credo, così affermo e così certo sono ad altra vita migliore dopo questa passare, là dove quella gloriosa donna vive de la quale fu l'anima mia innamorata quando contendea . . .'.

while figura is often inseparable from straightforward allegory, and was often interpreted as an aspect of allegory rather than as a wholly distinct device, it nonetheless implies an affirmation of the living reality of the figura, underlying the figured meaning that completes it, which allegory as such does not.[28]

At the opening of *Convivio* II Dante, in some much-discussed paragraphs about allegory,[29] distinguishes the allegory of poets from that of theologians. The only point in this passage that I wish to focus on here is the nature of Dante's example of poets' allegory, which is the kind he says he himself will employ. Poets use 'fictitious words' (*parole fittizie*): thus Ovid tells that Orpheus with his lute tamed beasts and made trees and rocks move. The truth hidden beneath this 'beautiful fiction' (*bella menzogna*) is that the wise man, with the instrument of his voice, can make cruel hearts gentle and move ignorant men according to his will.[30]

It is often claimed that poets' allegory deals with fictitious personages and events while theologians' allegory deals with biblical — that is, historical — ones.[31] Yet in relation to Dante at least this claim is seriously misleading, since Dante undoubtedly saw Orpheus as a historical figure, not a fictitious one. His

[28] Erich Auerbach, 'Figura', in his *Gesammelte Aufsätze zur romanischen Philologie* (Berne-Munich, 1967), pp. 55-92, esp. p. 77.

[29] *Conv.* II, i, 2-15. On the rather different account of allegory in the 'Epistle to Cangrande', and the reasons for doubting whether that account too could be by Dante, I abide by what I wrote in *Dante and Medieval Latin Traditions* (Cambridge, 1986), esp. pp. 103-11, notwithstanding Robert Hollander's *Dante's Epistle to Cangrande* (Ann Arbor, 1993), esp. pp. 43-53. In brief, the pattern of rhythmic cadences (*cursus*) in Dante's Latin expository prose, as in *De vulgari eloquentia* and *Monarchia*, is so markedly different from that in the expository part of the 'Epistle to Cangrande' that this is not likely to be by the same author.

If one looks at Hollander's polemic against this observation, it is significant that he has not tried to take account of Tore Janson's work on ascertaining where *cursus* is intentionally present in Latin prose and where it can — even if present in large proportions — be the result of coincidence (*Prose Rhythm in Medieval Latin*, Stockholm, 1975). Janson's groundbreaking study of this has meant that since 1975 all problems regarding the presence of *cursus* in Latin prose such as Dante's can be discussed far more precisely than was possible in previous scholarship. While Hollander alludes to 'Tore Janson 1975' (pp. 43 n. 1, 51 n. 15), he mentions the book only as a work used by other scholars, not as one he has used himself. Indeed he does not appear to realize that Janson's method is different from trying to count *percentages* of rhythmic cadences, as other scholars have attempted (and still attempt). Today there is little point in debating questions of *cursus* with those who have not assimilated Janson's notation and procedures: it would be rather like trying to debate the origin of species with fundamentalists who have not taken cognizance of Darwin.

I gave Professor Janson my excursus on Dante and prose rhythm to read before my 1986 book was published, and was delighted when he confirmed to me that the technical aspects of my discussion there were sound.

In his recent edition, *Epistola a Cangrande* (Florence, 1995), Enzo Cecchini (p. viii) defends the compatibility of the expository part with Dante's prose by the claim that it is a commentary, not a treatise like *De vulgari eloquentia*, and that one should not expect any systematic presence of *cursus* in a commentary. This is an arguable position, yet that one and the same author should, just this once, show no trace whatever of his lifelong rhythmic habits would still seem to me surprising.

[30] *Conv.* II, i, 3.

[31] Cf. *Fabula* (cit. n. 3), p. 119 n. 3.

ontological status is not that of, say, Medusa or the Graces: Orpheus is one of Dante's group of virtuous non-Christian sages in limbo — a group that begins with Aristotle, Socrates and Plato, and concludes with Hippocrates, Avicenna, Galen and Averroes (*Inf.* 4, 130 ff.).

Yet Ovid was able to use fictitious words and create a beautiful fiction about the historical Orpheus — a fiction capable of bearing an allegorical meaning. That is, if we adopt Auerbach's distinction, Orpheus is a figura, with his own vital narrative reality, rather than simply a pretext for an allegorical exemplification of the power of wisdom. In just this way, I would suggest, the Florentine girl who gazed at the grieving Dante with such compassion from her window, and whose face reminded him a little of Beatrice's, has her own vital narrative reality. And thus, when this noble young woman became for Dante a figura of Philosophy, this was imaginatively far more penetrating than his simply turning to a personified abstraction, an edifying allegorical substitute for a concept, would have been. The Donna Gentile as Philosophy 'does not exclude the Florentine girl who consoled Dante for Beatrice's death, but presupposes her: the beauty is that Dante is thus able to record what is both an earthly experience and a transcendent one'.[32] While I deliberately used the word 'experience', the human content of this concept must naturally remain open: how far the conflict with the memory of Beatrice, the wicked desire, the shame and the repentance, are *parole fittizie* and no more is something that (short of discovering wholly new evidence) we are unlikely ever to know.

Again there is a contradiction, which Nardi was not slow to underline: in the *Vita Nuova* the 'wicked desire' lasted for some days (*alquanti die*) and was then crushed; in the *Convivio* it grows and claims Dante's full allegiance in the course of 'perhaps thirty months'.[33] Once more it is a contradiction that must in some way be met without fudging. I have at least a small suggestion about what — imaginatively, rather than biographically — might lie behind it.

For Dante knew, from Boethius himself, that Philosophia *can* be desired in a base way, as well as in a noble one. When Philosophia first appears to Boethius, he sees that 'the hands of certain violent men had torn her dress, and each had seized whatever pieces he could'.[34] She, 'the mistress of all virtues', had been mishandled as if she were a prostitute. Soon Philosophia asks Boethius: 'Do you think this is the first time that Wisdom has been endangered by wanton behaviour?' The warring mob of Epicureans and Stoics who tore pieces off her dress thought on that account, she continues, 'that I had yielded to them totally' (*totam me sibi cessisse*); 'they were rashly imagined to be my intimates (*meos esse familiares*)'.[35] Even more strikingly, when Philosophia appears as a

[32] My formulation in *Medieval Latin and the Rise of European Love-Lyric* (2nd ed., 2 vols., Oxford, 1968), I, 95.

[33] *Conv.* II, xii, 7.

[34] *Cons. Phil.* (Loeb) I pr. 1, 22-24.

[35] Ibid. I pr. 3, 15-29.

sublimely radiant courtly *Domna* to Boecis, in the fragmentary Provençal poem of ca. 1070, she tells the prisoner:

> Many young men harass me,
> thinking that I will do their pleasure.
> First they love me, then they start hating me —
> so basely do they squander their love for me.[36]

If, as I believe, some of the connotations — the invisibles shown by the visible Florentine *consolatrix* — in the *Vita Nuova* already point in the direction of the fully imagined Filosofia of the *Convivio*, then we may well be able to distinguish the moment Dante describes in *Vita Nuova* XXXIX — 'my heart began dolorously to repent of the desire by which it had let itself be so basely possessed for some days, against the constancy of reason' — from the way in which, in the *Convivio*, his love for the Donna Gentile gradually became perfect, 'in a short time, perhaps thirty months' (*in picciol tempo, forse di trenta mesi*). In *Vita Nuova* XXXVIII, as we saw, Dante had distinguished between the object of his love, who was noble, and his thought about her, which he declared was — at least for some days — *vilissimo*. From this it might even be possible to speculate that, for some brief time near their beginning, Dante's philosophical studies, however ardent, were not purely disinterested — and that he then came to recognize that some element (of vanity, for example, or of political ambition) had been leading him towards philosophically false positions. And the savage outbursts in the fourth treatise of the *Convivio* remind us how passionately Dante cared about what he saw as philosophical falsehoods: in IV, xiv, for instance, of a hypothetical argument about nobility — that in the rest of creation it signifies intrinsic goodness, but among humans merely that a man's base ancestry has been forgotten — Dante exclaims 'One would want to reply not with words but with a knife to such a bestiality!' Such a moment suggests that Dante might as readily have accused himself of a philosophical as of a sensual transgression, even if this lasted only 'some days' in the course of 'perhaps thirty months' in the Donna Gentile's service.

The imagined conflict between rival loves is also touched upon in some of Dante's *rime* outside *Vita Nuova* and *Convivio*. The best known instance is in two sonnets that form a diptych, the one being the negation or palinode of the other.[37]

[36] *Boecis*, ed. René Lavaud, Georges Machicot (Toulouse, 1950), vv. 195-98:

> Molt me derramen — donzellet de jovent,
> Que zo espéren — que faza a lor talen.
> Primas me ámen, pois me van aïssent;
> La mí' amor — ta mal van deperden.

[37] Foster-Boyde nos. 62-63:

> Parole mie che per lo mondo siete,
> voi che nasceste poi ch'io cominciai
> a dir per quella donna in cui errai:

In the first, *Parole mie*, Dante addresses the songs he has already composed for the Donna Gentile: he refers explicitly within this sonnet to *Voi che 'ntendendo*, but most scholars agree that the poems Dante alludes to here include also the next canzone in the *Convivio*, *Amor che nella mente mi ragiona*, and the ballata *Voi che savete*, which laments the Donna Gentile's scornfulness. I shall return to these two in some detail in the next chapter.

In *Parole mie* Dante summons this group of songs — 'you that have gone through the world' (at a time, we must suppose, before the *Convivio* was written) — songs born in the period when he began to compose 'for that lady in whom I erred' (*per quella donna in cui errai*). This phrase is enigmatic, and has provoked diverse interpretations: that Dante was wrong to set the goal of his love in her; or that, having done so, he was deceived in her; or that, after seeming loving, she turned out to be disdainful; or again, that he erred in some aspect of his pursuit of philosophy; or finally (Contini's suggestion), that *in cui errai* here simply means 'on account of whom I suffered'.

Dante bids the existing Donna Gentile songs to go to her, 'crying out so that she hear your woes': in the context, this suggests that the songs themselves shall lament at ever having been composed for her. They are to say 'We are yours, but you shall never see any more songs like us' — Dante, that is, will never again compose lyrics for his second beloved. Then he bids them not to stay with the

'Voi che 'ntendendo il terzo ciel movete',
andatevene a lei, che la sapete
chiamando sì ch'ell'oda i vostri guai;
ditele: 'Noi siam vostre, ed unquemai
più che noi siamo non ci vederete'.
Con lei non state, ché non v'è Amore;
ma gite a torno in abito dolente
a guisa de le vostre antiche sore.
Quando trovate donna di valore,
gittatelevi a' piedi umilemente,
dicendo: 'A voi dovem noi fare onore.'

*

O dolci rime che parlando andate
de la donna gentil che l'altre onora,
a voi verrà, se non è giunto ancora,
un che direte: 'Questi è nostro frate.'
Io vi scongiuro che non l'ascoltiate,
per quel signor che le donne innamora,
ché ne la sua sentenzia non dimora
cosa che amica sia di veritate.
E se voi foste per le sue parole
mosse a venire inver la donna vostra,
non v'arrestate, ma venite a lei.
Dite: 'Madonna, la venuta nostra
è per raccomandarvi un che si dole,
dicendo: "Ov'è 'l disio de li occhi miei?"'

Donna Gentile but to go, dressed in robes of grief, back to Beatrice, and to prostrate themselves before her, saying 'It is you whom we must honour'. Whatever songs had been composed for his second love should, like a band of women in mourning, revert to his first, humbling themselves and paying homage to her instead.

The other sonnet in the diptych, *O dolci rime*, wittily belies its predecessor. Dante now warns the Donna Gentile songs that 'to you will come — if indeed he hasn't already — someone of whom you'll say "This is a brother of ours": I adjure you, don't listen to him!'. Dante calls his songs 'daughters', 'sisters', or (in the case of *sonetti*, which are grammatically masculine) 'brothers'.[38] He bids the songs for his second love, in the name of the Lord Amore, to reject what this treacherous false brother — the sonnet he has just composed — will tell them.

The train of thought in the sestet of *O dolci rime* is subtle and requires a certain collaboration from reader or listener. Dante tells the Donna Gentile songs: If the false brother's words have moved you to approach your lady, don't stop, but come to her. In *Parole mie*, these very songs had been commanded to go to Beatrice and implore her forgiveness for not having honoured her from the outset. Now the underlying idea would seem to be that the words of that sonnet, that specious brother, could only have the opposite effect from the one which was intended: instead of sending the Donna Gentile songs back in mourning and humility to Beatrice, the deceitful sonnet-brother will merely have frightened his sisters and left them taking shelter and comfort with the gentle lady to whom they truly belong. The word Dante twice uses here — *venire*, *venite* ('come', rather than 'go') — assumes a point of view that is the Donna Gentile's. The songs are told to come to her, not go to her — implying that she is not just their destination but their home. And when they come, they are to commend Dante to her anew: Dante in all his grief, and his longing for this, his second love — the man who, missing her, cries out, 'Where is the desire of my eyes?' *'Ov'è 'l disio de li occhi miei?'*.

The skirmish between the two loves, which concludes with this cry, is here acted out — in a deliberately more artful, playful fashion than in *Voi che 'ntendendo* — at a time when Dante has evidently already written several songs in praise of his second love. In the *Convivio*, having fully revealed her hidden meaning and nature — Filosofia, daughter of God and queen of all — it becomes easy for him to defend himself against the charge of unfaithfulness:

> . . . I thought I would perhaps be reproached for fickleness by many people in times to come, when they heard that I had changed from my first love; so, to clear away such a reproach, there was no better argument than to tell what the lady was like who had caused the change in me. For, by way of her manifest excellence one can contemplate her power, and by understanding the supreme magnitude of her power, one can recognize

[38] See Foster-Boyde II, 184.

that any stability of mind is mutable compared with that, and hence not judge me fickle or unstable.[39]

Have we with these words reached a more serious, more definitive position, beyond the dialectic of the sonnets? Is it only the existence of the *Commedia*, with its triumphant revindication of Beatrice, which makes us doubt that we have? It has been suggested in recent times that the change from the first to the second love was existentially so profound that when Dante, returning with all his being to the memory of Beatrice, embarked on the *Commedia*, he considered the *Convivio* 'no longer worthy of diffusion, let alone completion':[40] that 'the four treatises of the *Convivio* drafted by Dante remained among his private papers', and 'only after his death did someone make from the scribbled autograph, probably hard to read because of the provisional state in which the author had left it, that flawed copy on which the manuscripts which have come down to us depend'.

This hypothesis of Enzo Quaglio's, cited by Maria Corti in 1983 as 'perhaps the most plausible',[41] seems to me to suffer from precisely the same flaw as that of the lost earlier *Vita Nuova*. Underlying both hypotheses is a certain blurring conflation of biographical and artistic integrity, and a longing for a consistency that, constructed from the work, should pertain equally to the life. Yet in particular the pair of sonnets *Parole mie* and *O dolci rime* suggests to me that Dante was deliberately too spry for his future critics and their notions of consistency. His intellectual and imaginative play could be serious, passionate or poignant, and still be play. Some of Dante's poet-friends will happily have followed him into the more complex reaches of his poetic-dramatic fictions, and been in some measure his accomplices there. As we shall see, Dante can show keen awareness of the question of inconsistency in his writing: in the final strophe of the song *Amor che nella mente mi ragiona*, which opens *Convivio* III, he stresses that this song appears to contradict its sister, the ballata *Voi che savete ragionar d'Amore*, which had described the gentle lady as fierce and scornful. Dante goes on painstakingly to explain the grounds for the seeming inconsistency. If, likewise in the *Convivio*, he refers repeatedly to the *Vita Nuova* and never once intimates that there may be any incompatibility with that work, this was assuredly not an omission due to carelessness. Dante left the challenge with his poet-friends, with his first readers, and with us, the 'many people in

[39] *Conv.* III, i, 11-12: 'Dico che pensai che da molti, di retro da me, forse sarei stato ripreso di levezza d'animo, udendo me essere dal primo amore mutato; per che, a torre via questa riprensione, nullo migliore argomento era che dire quale era quella donna che m'avea mutato. Ché, per la sua eccellenza manifesta, avere si può considerazione de la sua virtude; e per lo 'ntendimento de la sua grandissima virtù, si può pensare ogni stabilitade d'animo essere a quella mutabile e però me non giudicare lieve e non stabile'.

[40] Cf. *La felicità mentale* (cit. n. 5), p. 154.

[41] Ibid. p. 155 (citing Quaglio verbatim).

times to come', of whom, precisely in the passage about those who might suspect him of fickleness, he showed himself aware.

The allusion to that future public, the many people in times to come, itself seems to me to weaken drastically the hypothesis that Dante relegated this incomplete work to his private papers as something unworthy of diffusion. Rather, he expected much both of his immediate and his future readers. He expected them to ponder his first and his second love, and, if they thought to see inconsistencies which he hadn't himself pointed out, to ponder yet again. At least a part of his artistic originality lay in his refusal to harmonize.

To illuminate this point further, by way of conclusion, I should like to venture on a comparison. In 1919 the Spanish Arabist Miguel Asín Palacios pointed out that at the beginning of the thirteenth century, in Murcia, the great mystic Ibn al-'Arabi had more than once used a prosimetric form in a way comparable to Dante's in the *Convivio*.[42] In Ibn al-'Arabi's major work, the *Futuhat*, each chapter is headed by a poem that gives an epitome of the topic which is then unfolded in the prose. Yet the closest parallel to the *Convivio* lies in a shorter work, *The Interpreter of Loves* (*Tarjuman al-Ashwaq*), a collection of odes that appear to be celebrations of human love. For each of these odes, in a complementary commentary, *The Treasures of Precious Things* (*Dhakha'ir al-a'laq*), the author shows in detail the allegorical mystical meanings hidden in the poetic language and imagery. The cycle of fifty-six odes was completed in January 1215 AD, the mystical commentary on them in August of that year.[43]

In taking up once more and trying to extend Asín's comparison, there is naturally no question of endorsing his underlying central argument — that Dante himself had direct access to Arabic sources which had not been translated into Latin or another western language. Though this, the basic thesis of Asín's famous study, *La escatología musulmana en la Divina Comedia*, has had to be rejected, his detailed comparisons between the *Commedia* and the 'Book of the Ascent', which relates Mohammad's otherworld journey, have proved immensely fruitful — especially since 1949, when it was discovered that this legendary work existed not only in Arabic but in a Latin translation and an Old French one, both made in the 1250s, as well as in an epitome in Castilian.[44] There was, however, no

[42] *La escatología musulmana en la Divina Comedia* (Madrid, 1919). For convenience I give in parenthesis page-references to the fourth edition (Madrid, 1984), which is a photographic reprint, with added material, of the second (Granada, 1943), published a year before the author's death. The 1943 and later editions differ from the first chiefly in adopting a different system for transliterating Arabic words and names. I use a simplified form of transliteration in what follows below. Asín's section on Ibn al-'Arabi comes on pp. 334-53 of the first edition, pp. 399-421 of the later ones.

[43] R. A. Nicholson (ed. and tr.), *The Tarjumán al-Ashwáq* (London, 1911), p. 6. In his notes, Nicholson includes abridged translations from the commentary, whose title he renders as *The Treasures of Lovers*.

[44] The western versions were edited with an outstanding introduction by Enrico Cerulli, *Il 'Libro della scala'* (Vatican City, 1949); the Latin version has been re-edited with a modern French facing translation by Gisèle Besson and Michèle Brossard-Dandré, *Le livre de l'échelle de Mahomet* (Paris, 1991). This includes relevant bibliography as far as 1990 (pp. 73-76).

comparable mediation to Christian culture of the works of Ibn al-'Arabi; hence Asín's chapter on him, near the close of *La escatología*, has been largely neglected in more recent times, even by those scholars who have gone back with profit to the earlier part, his very full account of the 'Book of the Ascent'. If we divide Asín's title for this last chapter into two — the first half, 'The close analogies between Dante and the Murcian mystic Ibn al-'Arabi', points to an insight that is still of exceptional value; the second half of the title, claiming that the analogies 'prove the hypothesis of imitation' (i.e. that Dante read and imitated the Arabic poet) is wholly far-fetched. Analogies, not imitations, will be the focus in what follows.

The motive for undertaking a commentary on the songs of love is, in both cases, an *excusatio*, in which the poet's longing to teach is inseparable from that of clearing himself of possible blame. Dante near the opening of his *Convivio* (I, ii, 15-17) says:

> I am moved to write both by the fear of loss of reputation and by the desire to impart instruction such as another cannot really give. I fear loss of reputation for having pursued so great a passion, as whoever reads the songs I have mentioned imagines held sway over me; this loss of reputation will entirely cease through what I say of myself here, which shows that not passion but virtue was the moving cause. I also intend to show the true meaning of those songs, which in some respects cannot be seen unless I relate it, because it is hidden beneath a figure of allegory.

Dante later adds, as we saw (II, xii, 8), that among the reasons he showed his condition 'under the figure of other things' was that his listeners 'would indeed have believed [him] capable of the first [i.e. human] love, but not of the second'.

Ibn al-'Arabi, in the prologue to his commentary on the odes of love, says:[45]

> The cause that moved me to compose this allegorical commentary on my songs was that my two spiritual sons . . . consulted me about them. And this because both had heard some ethical teachers in the city of Aleppo refusing to recognize that theological mysteries were concealed in my songs, adding that the Master was drawing a veil on account of his reputation for holiness and devotion. So I began to write a commentary on them . . . and when one of those who had refused to believe me heard me reading a part of it, he repented before God and corrected the malevolent judgement he had formed about mystic poets, with their amorous and youthful phrases by which they aim to express theological mysteries. I then set myself the task of completing these pages . . . alluding to transcendental intuitions, divine illuminations, spiritual mysteries, intellectual sciences and moral admonitions. And if to express all this I made use of the language characteristic of amorous and youthful poetry, it was so that men's souls, fond as they are of such dalliances, would thus have to feel themselves more drawn to hearing my songs.

[45] Asín pp. 342-33 (pp. 408-10); *Dhakha'ir al-a'laq*, ed. M. 'A. al-Kurdi (Cairo, 1968), pp. 3-7.

Equally remarkable in the light of the *Vita Nuova*, however, is Ibn al-'Arabi's affirmation, a little earlier in his prologue, that these songs were in the first instance inspired by a young woman who was as beautiful as she was holy: the poet's teacher in Mecca in the year 1201

had a daughter, a slender girl who held bound the gaze of whoever beheld her, and whose very presence graced our gatherings and dazed any person who saw her. Her name was Harmony, and her surname Eye of the Sun and of Beauty. Wise and filled with devotion and spirituality, in herself she personified the venerable antiquity of all the Holy Land and the fresh youthfulness of the great city loyal to the Prophet . . .[46] If there were no pusillanimous spirits ready to see scandal and disposed to think ill, I would here go on to reflect on the beauties with which God graced her, in her body as in her soul, which was a garden of nobility . . .

During the time that I was in her company, I observed carefully the noble gifts that adorned her person . . . Then I took her as the figure of inspiration for the poems this book contains — and these are love-poems, composed of beautiful and tender phrases, though I have not succeeded in expressing even a part of the emotion that my soul experienced, which intimacy with this young girl aroused in my heart, or of the noble love I felt for her, of the imprint her constant friendship left in my memory, of the grace of her spirit or the modesty of her bearing, since she, that most pure maiden, is the object of my quest and of my hope . . . But this is not all: in the verses I composed for this book I allude continually to divine inspirations, to spiritual visitations, and to relationships with the celestial Intelligences, conforming to our allegorical style — because to me the otherworld is better than this world, and because of her knowledge of what I was alluding to.

All this Ibn al-'Arabi mentions in the course of prefacing his commentary. Perhaps more startling still is that the commentary itself begins with a vision of a second beautiful woman, who is not Arabic, like his teacher's daughter in Mecca, but Greek. One night, during his ritual walk around the temple of the Ka'aba, composing some verses and reciting them aloud, the poet says:

I felt on my shoulder the touch of a hand softer than silk. I turned and found myself in the presence of a young Greek girl. Never had I beheld a woman with a lovelier face, with gentler speech, with more affectionate heart, with more spiritual thoughts, more subtle symbolic allusions, more elegant and gracious conversation. She surpassed all the women of her time in fineness of understanding, culture, beauty and wisdom.[47]

[46] On counterparts to this topos in the western tradition, cf. E. R. Curtius's section, 'Old Woman and Girl', in his *European Literature and the Latin Middle Ages* (tr. W. R. Trask, London, 1953), Ch. 5, sect. 9, pp. 101-05 (= *Europäische Literatur und lateinisches Mittelalter*, 2nd ed., Berne, 1954, 'Greisin und Mädchen', pp. 112-15).

[47] Asín p. 344 (p. 411). For the second and third passages of Ibn al-'Arabi cited above, I was also able to consult the translation by Henry Corbin, in his *L'imagination créatrice dans le soufisme d'Ibn 'Arabî* (Paris, 1958), pp. 104 f., 107. For all three passages, I am deeply grateful to Charles Burnett for notes and advice about nuances of meaning in the Arabic original.

It is the second, Greek girl who, in the commentary, is allegorized, not the Arabic girl who had originally inspired the songs. The Greek one becomes an allegory of divine Wisdom, her smile stands for the illuminations of supernatural knowledge, her gaze signifies the power of light and demonstration.[48]

Some of the imagery in the cycle of odes[49] shows special affinities with the *Vita Nuova*, some with the *Convivio*. In one ode (IV), the beloved causes the poet-lover distress by withholding her greeting from him,[50] but then she reveals the lightning-flash of her smile.[51] In another (XX), where she is described as 'endowed with prose and verse', the commentary makes explicit that this 'tender playful girl' is 'a form of Divine Wisdom, essential and holy, which fills the heart with joy'.

In yet another ode (XXIII), Ibn al-'Arabi invokes a group of pilgrims:[52] 'Oh you who travel on this road, look on us again with pity! For we were robbed, a little after dawn, a little before sunrise, of a bright-faced lissome girl'. The commentary explains that the girl is an attribute of the divine essence, lissome in her descent towards humanity, and that her sudden disappearance means that she remains inaccessible and unknown to human understanding.

Lest I seem to be pressing Dantesque resemblances one-sidedly, I should perhaps also mention that much of the imagery in these odes is characteristically Arabic and far from Dante's: it includes many images of camels and camel-drivers, the desert and its wells, peacocks, perfumes, howdahs; moreover, quite a few of the poems speak not just of one young woman who stands for Divine Wisdom, but of a plurality of women, who are interpreted in the commentaries as blessed spirits or as divine names. Yet the passages that show analogies with Dante are likewise numerous, and I do not wish to pass over entirely two others that seem to me exceptional, one in relation to the *Convivio*, the other to the *Vita Nuova*.

In his prologue, Ibn al-'Arabi had declared that the name of the beautiful girl in Mecca who had inspired his love-songs and his spiritual passion was Harmony. In one of the odes (XXIX) he develops this thought: the 'slender girl who

[48] Asín p. 344 n. 1 (p. 411 n. 1), citing *Dhakha'ir* 78, 21 and 33 respectively.

[49] References in what follows are to the odes as numbered in Nicholson's edition; citations in English are after Nicholson.

[50] Compare *VN* X, 2.

[51] Compare *Amor che nella mente mi ragiona* (Foster-Boyde no. 61), vv. 63 ff., where the Donna Gentile's 'beauty rains down flames of fire . . . and like a flash of lightning these shatter the innate vices that make people base'. The commentaries I have seen (Foster-Boyde, Barbi-Pernicone, and De Robertis in *Convivio*) have not remarked on what I believe ultimately underlies this paradox of beauty that is devastating in its effects: the passage in Cant. 6, 9 which in the Vulgate reads:

> Quae est ista quae progreditur quasi aurora consurgens,
> pulchra ut luna, electa ut sol,
> terribilis ut castrorum acies ordinata?

('Who is she who comes forth like the rising dawn, beautiful as the moon, peerless as the sun, terrible as a host in battle-array?')

[52] Compare the sonnet *Deh peregrini* (*VN* XL, 9-10) cited above.

bestowed favours and bounties' on him 'established the harmony of union, for she is our principle of harmony: she is both Arab and foreign'. The ideal projected here can hardly fail to call to mind the sublime moment in *Convivio* III, xiv, where it is shown that Filosofia herself generates the three virtues — faith, hope and charity — which lead human beings to rise in their speculation to a 'celestial Athens', where the conflicting schools of philosophers become one in mind and heart. And finally, Ibn al-'Arabi shares Dante's particular delight in analysing the mystic meaning of numbers in relation to his beloved: where Beatrice was 'a nine, that is, a miracle, whose root is solely the wondrous Trinity' (*VN* XXIX), the Arabic poet's love, 'exalted in majesty above Time', is 'a maid of fourteen' (XL); the commentary explains how this signifies 'the perfect soul': because 'four is the most perfect number, and ten consists of four numbers, 1 + 2 + 3 + 4, and fourteen is 4 + 10'.[53]

In Ibn al-'Arabi's cycle of odes, the *Tarjuman*, we sense that the poetry, as in the *Vita Nuova*, is charged with hidden meanings — that it is, in the Victorine terms, a gathering of visible forms to show *invisibilia*. At the same time, as in the *Convivio*, Ibn al-'Arabi provides in a prose commentary detailed allegorical readings, specifying what each expression signifies in its hidden sense. The motive claimed for this is, as we saw, very similar to that claimed by Dante: both to instruct and to clear oneself of the suspicion of involvement in a base human love. And yet, again as with Dante's allegorêsis in the *Convivio*, the prose that is meant to resolve the ambiguities serves rather to deepen them — especially in the moments, in both poet-commentators, where allegorêsis is enriched by elements of narrative.

It is above all these narrative elements that — probably with the premeditation and connivance of Ibn al-'Arabi as of Dante — tempt readers towards imaginings where poetic speculation blends with biographical. For instance: was Ibn al-'Arabi really inspired by two beautiful young women, virtuous and wise, the first of whom was Arabic, the second Greek? Or is the second purely a fictional device for introducing his commentary elegantly? Or are both perhaps only fictions? If there was an experiential as well as a fictive element, should we envisage this as a man's sublimation of a human love, or loves? Or should we imagine Ibn al-'Arabi as an ascetic using attractive rhetorical devices for spiritual ends, while in truth remaining impervious to human love? Or again, were his hostile critics perhaps right at least in this, that they saw traces of truly human eroticism in his songs — even if the holy man had persuaded himself he was completely free of these? Needless to say, I cannot even begin to answer any of these questions.

[53] Is it pure coincidence that the ode where this is expounded is set in the fortieth place (i.e. 4 × 10) in the *Tarjuman*?

One cannot go far wrong, however, in saying that in the situation of allegorizing a human love — whether Ibn al-'Arabi's or Dante's — there is something that remains inevitably slippery:

> . . . each venture
> Is a new beginning, a raid on the inarticulate
> With shabby equipment always deteriorating
> In the general mess of imprecision of feeling,
> Undisciplined squads of emotion.[54]

Yet beyond what is intrinsically ambiguous, in Ibn al-'Arabi and in Dante, there is also the conviction, essential to both these poet-commentators, that what they are aspiring to is intrinsically precious and so beyond censure. That Dante evolved further, and aspired to something different in his *Commedia*, does not affect this point in any way. To see the *Convivio* aright we must, at least for a time, read it as though there were no *Commedia*. If the incomplete work is, from one vantage-point, a transition, it can also, from another, be seen as a culmination.

[54] T. S. Eliot, *East Coker*, V.

II

THE DONNA GENTILE: *OBSCURIS VERA INVOLVENS*

The song *Amor che nella mente mi ragiona*, with which the third treatise of the *Convivio* opens, has its recognized place among the splendours of Dante's lyric poetry. It is one of his supreme achievements in the canzone form. That it is the song which his musician-friend Casella chooses to sing for Dante on the shore of Purgatory,[1] casting a spell over him and Vergil and all the souls that had come in the angel's ship, indicates how potent a place it held for Dante among his *rime*.[2] In *Amor che nella mente* there is intellectual fullness, but also tautness and compression; a controlled excitement underlies the verses and impels them. There is likewise an expressive fullness, the language moving towards hymnody in the central strophes, then passing gently into witty reflection in the concluding one. The song conjoins, in Coleridge's phrase, 'a more than usual state of emotion with more than usual order'.[3]

Yet there is another, quite different reason why I would see *Amor che nella mente* as occupying a unique place in the history of poetry: it is the only lyric I know, in any language, that finds its complete resplendence not alone but in the setting of its commentary. It is the imbrication in *Convivio* III of images and concepts, personal and metaphysical reminiscence, lyricism and ardent speculation, on which I wish to focus in some detail here. For it is through this imbrication that Dante achieves a structure, texture and design such as no poet working alone, and no philosopher working alone, has attempted or attained.

It is easy to say, easy to see, that Dante's Donna Gentile is, at least to some extent, a fusion of two earlier personified beings: Philosophia, who consoled Boethius, and Sapientia, who is celebrated in the 'Solomonic' books of the Old Testament. Naturally I shall not neglect or belittle either of these illustrious

1 *Purg.* 2, 112.

2 Much has been written about the significance of the choice of this song, and of Cato's rebuke of the assembled 'rapt and attentive' spirits (*Purg.* 2, 118-23). I am convinced by Lino Pertile's subtle recent interpretation of the episode ('Dante's Comedy beyond the *Stilnovo*', *Lectura Dantis*, 13, 1993, 47-77, esp. pp. 56-61): 'what Cato actually objects to is not the content of *Amor che ne la mente*, but rather the arresting effects of its musical sweetness'. At the imagined dramatic moment of 1300, before the *Convivio* was begun, the canzone has the semblance of a love-song borne on the highest flights of language of the *stilnovisti*, not of a celebration of Filosofia; thus 'Cato's rebuke is directed not to the pursuit of Lady Philosophy in the *Convivio*, but to Dante's indulgence in sweet poetry and song — and by implication in the practice of the *dolce stil novo* — at a time when he should be thinking of purging himself'. The early readers of Dante's *Commedia* could not have been expected to know the context in the *Convivio*, 'a work known only to himself'. See also the further discussion in the Excursus below.

3 *Biographia Literaria*, Ch. XIV, *ad fin.*: '[Imagination] reveals itself in the balance or reconcilement of opposite or discordant qualities . . . the idea with the image . . . a more than usual state of emotion with more than usual order; judgement ever awake and steady self-possession with enthusiasm and feeling profound or vehement . . .'.

ancestors of Dante's Donna, and I hope to bring certain new insights about how she is related to both. At the same time I should like to emphasize, far more than has been attempted hitherto, some of the ways in which the Donna Gentile differs from her Boethian and Solomonic prototypes: it is in these differences that Dante's originality gleams.

For the Donna Gentile is set in a profound and unusual metaphysical structure, which is not to be found in Boethius, and even less in the biblical passages, and which, notwithstanding all the learning that scholars — especially Nardi and Vasoli — have lavished on it,[4] cannot be reduced to any of the metaphysical sources that Dante cites, or to any combination of earlier source-materials. Dante's mind, moving in the midst of those materials unpredictably and eclectically, creates an astonishing personal conception. If we come with ready categories — Neoplatonic, Hermetic, Aristotelian; Avicennist, Averroist, Thomist; philosophical, theological, poetic — we gradually perceive that the vision underlying the canzone *Amor che nella mente*, and the whole third treatise of the *Convivio*, admits elements of all these, yet in its individuality also continually eludes them.

Boethius' Philosophia is a quasi-celestial consoler and instructress, yet ultimately she must be called human rather than celestial. If at times her head seems to touch heaven or even to penetrate heaven,[5] she is not, like Dante's projection, the being 'thought by him who moved the universe'.[6] Peter Abelard and Jean de Meun were at least partly right when they interpreted Philosophia as an aspect of Boethius' own consciousness[7] — its most commanding aspect, divinely irradiated, but not in her own right a cosmic figure, or a sharer of the divine mind, such as the Donna Gentile becomes in the canzone.

There, and throughout the *Convivio* commentary, the Donna Gentile is summoned up with an iridescent plenitude of detail; yet there is no dialogue with her, such as Boethius has with Philosophia. Dante imagines her too loftily to present her as his interlocutrix. The dramatic vivacity of dialogue between the poet-protagonist and his heavenly beloved — who can solace and instruct, but also show herself reproachful, scornful, possessive, or impatient at his mental slowness, as well as at times radiantly loving and tender, perfecting her devotee in sensibility and understanding — this range of dramatic possibilities, which Boethius adumbrated in his dialogues with Philosophia, was to be transformed

4 Bruno Nardi's principal contributions to the study of the meaning and intellectual background of the *Convivio* can be found gathered together in his three volumes (in chronological order), *Saggi di filosofia dantesca* ([Milan, 1930], 2nd ed., Florence, 1967); *Nel mondo di Dante* (Rome, 1944); and *Dal 'Convivio' alla 'Commedia'* (Rome, 1960). Cesare Vasoli's many insights are distilled in his commentary on the prose parts of the *Convivio* (cit. Ch. I n. 1), which in recent years I have consulted as steadily as Nardi's essays.

5 *Cons. Phil.* (Loeb) I pr. 1, 10-13.

6 *Amor che nella mente*, v. 72 (*costei pensò chi mosse l'universo*).

7 Cf. my discussion in *Verse with Prose: From Petronius to Dante* (Cambridge, Mass., 1994), pp. 40 f., where the relevant texts of Abelard and Jean de Meun are cited.

and intensified with the figure of Beatrice in the *Commedia*. We are *told* that the Donna Gentile can, through her flames of beauty, create all good thoughts and shatter innate vices like a flash of lightning —

> Sua bieltà piove fiammelle di foco,
> animate d'un spirito gentile
> ch'è creatore d'ogni pensier bono;
> e rompon come trono
> l'innati vizii che fanno altrui vile. (63-67)

Yet here in the *Convivio* there is nothing comparable to the narrative-dramatic parts of Boethius' *Consolation*: we are not *shown* how such effects come about.

Another difference from Boethius' figure is that the Donna Gentile's cosmic aspect — 'every Intelligence on high gazes upon her', 'she was established eternally'[8] — is accompanied by allusions to her specifically courtly qualities and allure: the sighs that her beauty arouses, the graciousness of her actions, the way she becomes an exemplar for the rest of womankind —

> gentile è in donna ciò che in lei si trova,
> e bello è tanto quanto lei simiglia. (49 f.)

> noble in woman is what is found in her,
> and beautiful whatever resembles her.

Where the Donna Gentile is, like the biblical Sapientia, the companion of God from eternity, Boethius' heroine demarcates herself clearly from God and the divine sphere. The one time that she uses words borrowed from those describing Sapientia in the Book of Wisdom, it is precisely to designate *not* herself but the Supreme Good, the *summum bonum*, which she apprehends but which lies beyond her. Where Sapientia (Wisdom 8, 1) 'spans mightily from one end to the other and disposes all things gently', Philosophia tells Boethius: 'It is the Supreme Good which rules all things mightily and disposes them all gently'.[9]

There is in fact a passage at the opening of another of Boethius' works where briefly he comes far closer to evoking and celebrating a figure comparable to the Donna Gentile and exalted in the manner of the biblical Sapientia. Since I cannot find that Dante scholars have taken account of this text — it opens Boethius' first commentary on Porphyry (not perhaps *prima facie* the most promising place to search) — I shall cite it in some detail:[10]

[8] *Amor che nella mente*, vv. 23, 54.

[9] *Cons. Phil.* III pr. 12, 63 f: *'Est igitur summum', inquit, 'bonum quod regit cuncta* fortiter suaviter*que* disponit'; cf. Sap. 8, 1: *'Attingit enim a fine usque ad finem* fortiter *et* disponit *omnia* suaviter'.

[10] Boethius, *In Porphyrium (Editio prima)*, ed. S. Brandt, CSEL 48.1 (Vienna, 1906), p. 7, lines 12-23 (punctuation and capitalization mine):

Philosophy is the love and pursuit and in a sense friendship of Wisdom — not of this wisdom which is found in certain arts and in the knowledge and notions of crafts, but of that great Wisdom who, in need of no one, is the vivacious mind and sole primordial reason of things.

Here love of Wisdom is the illumination of the understanding mind by that pure Wisdom, in which she in a sense draws and summons the mind back to herself, so that the pursuit of wisdom seems rather to be the pursuit of divinity and the friendship of her pure mind.

In every kind of soul this Wisdom therefore imprints the reward of her divinity, and leads each kind back to the power and purity inherent in her own nature. From this is born the truth of speculations and thoughts, and a holy and innocent purity of actions.

Here the divine aspect of Sapientia's rôle, and the human moral perfection achievable through the loving bond with her, emerge in a way that has no precise parallel in the more celebrated *Consolation of Philosophy*.

Let us now turn to consider how 'that great Wisdom' is introduced into Dante's argument.

At the opening of the canzone, the 'Love which speaks to me fervently in my mind about my lady' is no longer that personified Amore, that 'lord of dread aspect',[11] who had dominated the visions and dialogues in the *Vita Nuova*. Love here, and especially in the twofold commentary on the opening verses, becomes a key concept in Dante's new metaphysical structure, which, for all its learned range of reference, is strikingly individual in its total expression.

Love, the argument in the prose begins, is nothing other than the spiritual union of the soul and the object loved. Such a definition can be at home in various contexts, including a strictly Aristotelian one — there is a closely similar wording, for instance, in Thomas Aquinas's commentary on Aristotle's passage about Eros as a universal principle, at the beginning of the *Metaphysics*.[12] Dante, however, moves from this definition to an evocation of the Neoplatonic cosmos implied by the axioms in the *Liber de causis*, the gnomic compilation based on

Est enim philosophia amor et studium et amicitia quodammodo Sapientiae — sapientiae vero non huius, quae in artibus quibusdam et in fabrili scientia notitiaque versatur, sed illius Sapientiae, quae, nullius indigens, vivax mens et sola rerum primaeva ratio est.

Est autem hic amor Sapientiae intelligentis animi ab illa pura Sapientia inluminatio et quodammodo ad se ipsam retractio atque advocatio, ut videatur studium Sapientiae studium divinitatis et purae mentis illius amicitia.

Haec igitur Sapientia cuncto equidem animarum generi meritum suae divinitatis inponit et ad propriam naturae vim puritatemque reducit. Hinc nascitur speculationum cogitationumque veritas et sancta puraque actuum castimonia.

Strangely, Vasoli makes reference to this text, but cites (at p. 421 n. 6) only the opening words, defining philosophy, and mentions nothing further. In my view it is the passage that follows the definition (from *sapientiae vero non huius* onwards) which is truly remarkable and illuminating in relation to Dante.

[11] *VN* III, 3.

[12] *In Metaph.* I, 5, 102: 'That love unites things is clear from this, that love itself is a kind of union of the lover and what is loved, since the lover regards the beloved object as himself'.

Proclus, translated from the Arabic in the twelfth century, to which Dante turns as an authority on no fewer than five occasions in the *Convivio*.[13] There we are shown how all forms proceed from God, the transcendent first cause, by way of the Intelligences, who effect the human soul and the sublunary world. Each form, Dante explains, shares in some measure in the divine nature, the more so the nobler it is — the human soul most of all among sublunary things. The soul longs for being, and its being depends on God, so it longs to be united with God, and with the goodnesses that show themselves in nature.[14] The plural 'goodnesses' (Dante's *bontadi*, Latin *bonitates*) is one of the heart-words of the *Liber de causis*: from the highest to the lowest reaches of its cosmos, the Intelligences transmit divine effects, or *bonitates*, by which the unknowable divine being reveals itself to whatever degree created beings can receive its revelation. The union with the divine *bonitates* is love. And for Dante this love is the union of his soul with the Donna Gentile. This love, he therefore explains, is the speaker at the opening of his song, telling 'of this lady who had spiritually become one with my soul'.[15]

Here the pursuit of Wisdom, conceived in terms of a love-union through which a human being can attain divinity, is set within a universe in which all beings strive in their own modes to return to the first cause, to become 'as divine as possible'. This expression too is Aristotelian, yet the fervent vision of an ordered creation proceeding from a primal divine source and returning to it is unmistakably Neoplatonic. Boethius was no stranger to this notion: in the prayer *O qui perpetua*, set at the centre of his *Consolation of Philosophy*,[16] Philosophia evokes the cosmic procession and return unforgettably for the poet-prisoner. Yet it is important to remember that there she is voicing a prayer to God on Boethius' behalf — there is no question of Philosophia herself being the divine *bonitas* with whom Boethius will be united.

The mind, Dante declares soon afterwards, is the highest and noblest part of the human soul. It is that subtle and most precious part which is godhead (*deitade*). 'This is where Amore speaks to me about my lady'.[17] Here Dante goes on to expound how each being in creation has a love that is specific to it, whilst man, whose specific love is directed towards what is perfect and honourable, has a nature that can comprehend the loves of every grade of being.

[13] Four of Dante's five references (which are listed at Vasoli p. 924) occur in *Convivio* III, one in *Convivio* IV. According to Nardi, *Saggi* (cit. n. 4) p. 84, it is hard to establish from these references whether Dante knew the complete work at first hand, and it is more probable that he knew the commentary on the *De causis* by Albert the Great than that by Thomas Aquinas. At all events Dante was aware of the salient features of the *Liber*, and of some of its characteristic modes of expression (*bonitates*, *influxio*), of which he gives his individual vernacular renderings in the third treatise (see the discussion below).

[14] *Conv.* III, ii, 4-8.

[15] *Conv.* III, ii, 9.

[16] *Cons. Phil.* III m. 9; Dante translates the verses about cosmic procession at *Conv.* III, ii, 17.

[17] *Conv.* III, ii, 19.

In this passage there are two textual cruces: first, when Dante evokes the innate love of plants for the place where they will best grow with the words:[18] *e però vedemo certe piante lungo l'acque quasi cantarsi* ('and thus we see certain plants as it were singing to themselves[19] when they are alongside water'). Half a dozen different emendations have been proposed for *cantarsi*,[20] the word in the archetype — these would all, if adopted, have the effect of removing Dante's unusual metaphor. None of the emendations takes account of the force of *quasi*, the word that indicates Dante's consciousness of speaking metaphorically at this point.[21] Besides, the image of the plant's song, in precisely such a context, is at least as old as Proclus, who (in a passage probably not available to Dante in Latin) had written of

> beholding in heaven earthly things, in their cause and celestially, and on earth heavenly things terrestrially . . . If there were anyone who could hear how the heliotrope beats the air as it turns, in this sound he would perceive it sending forth to [God], its King, a canticle such as a plant can sing.[22]

The sentence by which Dante explains how mankind can have the motions of love proper to every degree of created being, has a further crux, and here one small emendation — though only one — does seem to be needed:

> E però che l'uomo, avvegna che una sola sustanza sia tutta *su*a forma, per la sua nobilitade ha in sé natura divina, queste cose, tutti questi amori, puote avere e tutti li ha. (III, iii, 5)

> And because the human being, though his whole form is one single substance, has a divine nature in himself because of his nobility, he can have these things — all these loves — and has them all.

This is how the sentence reads in the (deduced) archetype, except that it had *fia forma*, which an early corrector changed to *sua forma*, and which, in Vasoli's words, was 'a probable emendation, perhaps spontaneous, or perhaps derived

[18] *Conv.* III, iii, 4.

[19] I construe the reflexive pronoun *si* as a dative of favour — here, to do something for one's own benefit. I am grateful to Professor Giovanni Aquilecchia for advice on this point.

[20] Vasoli (pp. 318 f.) lists the conjectures *contentarsi* — which he himself prints, following the 1921 Società Dantesca edition — *piantarsi*, *confarsi*, *cansarsi*, *criarsi*, and *quas'incantarsi*. Ageno (p. 163) reverts to *cansarsi*.

[21] This was well seen by Maria Simonelli, *Materiali per un'edizione critica del 'Convivio' di Dante* (Rome, 1970), pp. 183 f., who argues for retaining *cantarsi*, 'un'immagine di per sé felicissima'. Yet, not aware of the Neoplatonic image of the plant singing, she assumes that the word 'forse non vuol indicare altro che una pienezza di vita'.

[22] The Greek original is given in *Catalogue des manuscrits alchimiques grecs* (Brussels, 1928), VI, 148. While I have not attempted an exhaustive search among the texts and testimonies of 'Proclus Latinus' available in the West by ca. 1300, I have not come across a Latin counterpart to this passage, earlier than the translation which Ficino made: 'Opus Procli de sacrificio et magia', ed. Wilhelm Kroll, *Analecta Graeca* (Greifswald, 1901), pp. 5-14.

from a codex closer to the [actual] archetype which today is lost'.[23] Apart from that, I wholly endorse Simonelli's argument[24] that no other retouching is necessary in this passage, and in particular, that the vital word *divina* — stressing the divine nature of the human being — must not be altered.[25] It is by virtue of nobility, the divine aspect of man, that his love for the whole of creation is possible.

The passage, I would suggest, echoes the joyous celebration of the human relation to nature and to divinity in the renowned Hermetic treatise, *Asclepius*, which Dante will have known either directly or by way of its many citations by Albert the Great. In *Asclepius* the human being, the *magnum miraculum*,[26] is given a 'worldly envelope' by the transcendent God, in order that he should love not only heavenly things but the created universe, 'binding it to himself by a knot of love . . . so that he who loves the things below him is himself loved by the heavenly ones'.[27]

The Neoplatonic image of a universe in which the Intelligences mediate the divine to the world below, begun in the second chapter of *Convivio* III, is dwelt upon more fully in the sixth and seventh, as Dante turns to explain the lines about the Donna Gentile:

> Ogni Intelletto di là su la mira,
> e quella gente che qui s'innamora
> ne' lor pensieri la truovano ancora
> quando Amor fa sentir de la sua pace. (23-26)
>
> Every Intelligence on high beholds her,
> and those who fall in love with her here below
> find her again in their thoughts
> when Love brings them a share of his peace.

The Intelligences apprehend the form of the Donna Gentile in God: in the divine mind she is the ideal representation of the human essence (*l'essemplo intenzionale che de la umana essenzia è ne la divina mente*).[28] The Intelligences that fashion the world below and transmit divine effects to it have implanted in

[23] Vasoli p. 319.

[24] *Materiali* (cit. n. 21) p. 185.

[25] Both Vasoli (p. 319) and Ageno (p. 163) change *natura divina* to *natura d'ognuna di*, which then governs the phrase *queste cose*.

[26] With this phrase compare especially *Conv.* III, viii, 1: *Intra li effetti de la divina sapienza l'uomo è mirabilissimo*.

[27] *Asclepius*, 6 (*Corpus Hermeticum*, ed. Nock-Festugière, Paris, 1960, II, 301 f.): ' . . . magnum miraculum est homo . . . cetera omnia, quibus se necessarium esse caelesti dispositione cognoscit, nexu secum caritatis adstringit . . . ut, quae infra se sunt, diligat, ipse a se superioribus diligatur'. (For the *mundanum integimentum*, cf. *Ascl.* 8, p. 305). On Albert and the *Hermetica*, cf. L. Sturlese, 'Saints et magiciens: Albert le Grand en face d'Hermès Trismégiste', *Archives de Philosophie*, 43 (1980), 615-34.

[28] *Conv.* III, vi, 6.

human beings the desire for a perfection in which the whole of their desire can be stilled. Again this sounds Aristotelian; and for a brief moment, when Dante adds that no delectation in this life is so great that it can fully still that implanted desire, we come close to Thomas Aquinas.[29] Yet almost immediately the argument takes on a wholly different colouring: she, the Donna Gentile, *is* the perfection that is desired by mankind. And more — she receives divine goodness superhumanly. The divine goodness streams into her, and from her into us. The word Dante uses for that streaming or outpouring, *discorrimento*, is the precise equivalent of the key expression *influxio* in the *Liber de causis*, which Dante cites at this moment: 'The primal Goodness sends its goodnesses over things in a single outpouring'.[30] Beings are diversely capable of receiving these goodnesses, just as there are diverse capacities of receiving the sun's light, with mirrors at the one extreme of receptiveness and solid earth at the other. When Dante says that angels are the most diaphanous to the divine light, he is adapting a beautiful image from pseudo-Dionysius' *On the Divine Names*:

> an angel is . . . a pure mirror, most resplendent . . . receiving the whole loveliness of well-formed deiformity and purely declaring that goodness in himself as far as possible.[31]

Yet when Dante adds that the human being has a part that is free of matter and another that is impeded by it, his language leaves the buoyant optimism of the Dionysian sacramental universe for a more sombre Platonic dualism, in which matter does not reveal spirit but weighs spirit down. Then, as he explains that the hierarchy of being is a continuum, in which the basest humans seem almost like beasts, and the noblest like angels, Dante turns once more to the *auctoritas* of Aristotle: it is these angel-like human beings whom Aristotle in the *Ethics* calls divine.[32]

The purpose of this *auctoritas*, however, is one that would have left Aristotle himself stupefied: it is to explain why divine power descends into the Donna Gentile as into an angel. And Dante's seventh chapter culminates in an audacious argument that is wholly unprecedented — as far from Aristotle and the

[29] *Conv.* III, vi, 7. Cf. Thomas Aquinas, *Contra Gentiles*, III, 48 (the Latin is cited more fully by Vasoli ad loc.): 'The ultimate goal of man ends his natural desire in such a way that, possessing it, nothing else is sought . . . But that cannot happen in this life . . . Thus it is not possible for the ultimate felicity of man to exist in this life'.

[30] *Conv.* III, vii, 2.

[31] *De div. nom.* 4 (Eriugena's Latin version, P. L. 122, 1141): 'angelus est . . . speculum purum, splendidissimum . . . recipiens totam . . . speciositatem bene formatae deiformitatis, et pure declarans in seipso, sicut possibile est, bonitatem'.

[32] *Conv.* III, vii, 6-7; cf. Aristotle, *Eth.* VII, 1, 1145a, 11-25. Even closer, perhaps, is the abridged adaptation of the *Ethics*, *Liber Ethicorum*, that was used by Brunetto Latini (ed. Concetto Marchesi, *L'Etica Nicomachea nella tradizione latina medievale*, Messina, 1904, p. lxviii): *et tales homines angelici dicuntur sive divini propter intensionem virtutis in ipsis*. This version, like the *Convivio* passage, includes the word 'angelic', which does not feature here either in the Latin text of the *Ethics* or in Thomas Aquinas's commentary.

Neoplatonists as from anything in medieval Scholasticism: The countenance (*aspetto*) of the Donna Gentile, he affirms, helps Christian faith. Since many people persist in a fog of doubt about Christ's miracles, and cannot believe in any miracle without having experience of it visibly, she is the visibly miraculous being whom we can behold each day, and thereby she makes us see other miracles as possible.

Dante, that is, now claims for the Donna Gentile precisely that status of incarnate divine miracle, blessed in her effects, which he had claimed for Beatrice in the *Vita Nuova*. It would be easy to paraphrase this remarkable, extravagant affirmation unsympathetically and baldly: for instance: 'We can look at a page of philosophy each day, and find this so marvellous that then we'd be disposed to believe anything'. Yet this would be to make oneself deaf (or blind) to the connotations of the womanly mediatrix of the highest truths, Dante's personal transformation of the Solomonic Sapientia.

Equally daring and original is the allegorical exposition of the way in which the Donna Gentile's beauty creates faith: as Filosofia can show us through reason much that without her help seems a marvel (*maraviglia*), so through her one can believe that any miracle (*ogni miracolo*) can have its reason in a higher intellect, and this second conviction can give rise to faith.[33] It has not, I think, been noticed that underlying this argument is the twofold process of symbolic perception which Dante knew through pseudo-Dionysius, and which he had explained succinctly in Chapter xii. There he affirmed that, first, it is appropriate to treat intelligible realities, which are beyond sense-perception, by way of sensory images. But the second, complementary aspect is to treat supra-intelligible realities (the *inintelligibili* that surpass our intellection as well as our perception) by way of intelligible ones — by way of the angels or Intelligences, or, in Dante's thought above all, the Donna Gentile. She, our visible miracle, who dwells in the divine realm, can lead us to a faith in the *inintelligibili* which is not anti-rational, but is an inference, or symbolic perception, analogous to the one that moves from the sensible to the intelligible, so often ventured on both by poets and philosophers. A faith in the transcendent arrived at in this way, so the argument in III, xiv continues, gives rise to hope and to charity.

Though the way Dante expresses all this and the way he arrives at it are wholly unusual, one might still up to this point imagine that the abstract equivalent of what he is saying is not so different from the thought of someone such as Thomas Aquinas. Thomas, as is well known, sees reason as capable of providing a certain foundation for and help towards faith: philosophy (which can legitimately treat such matters as the existence of God and the nature of the soul) can become the handmaiden (*ancilla*) of theology, the harbinger of faith (*praeambula fidei*), walking ahead like a page-girl to light her mistress's way. Yet for Dante this is not the end of the story. For him the faith and hope and charity

[33] *Conv.* III, xiv, 14.

which the Donna Gentile, the living miracle, can inspire, lead not to theology but to a new *philosophical* accord:

Through these three virtues we rise, to philosophize, to that celestial Athens, where the Stoics and Peripatetics and Epicureans, through the light of eternal truth, concur concordantly in one single intent (*in uno volere concordevolemente concorrono*).[34]

In this wholly unparalleled vision of a philosophical utopia — a heaven of reason, rather than of theology's saints and angels — Dante extends his ecumenic welcome more widely than even his beloved Boethius would have done. For Boethius, Stoics and Epicureans were among the unworthy lovers who had torn Philosophia's dress. Dante, instead, shows an unbounded optimism: the love which the Donna Gentile can inspire will lead to concord, even among those whose philosophies had conflicted on earth. The passage foreshadows Dante's equally independent, equally magnanimous evocation in *Paradiso*, of Thomas Aquinas paying tribute to the truth of his adversary Siger of Brabant, Bonaventure to that of his adversary Joachim of Fiore.[35]

When Dante expounds the allegory of the Donna Gentile as Filosofia,[36] he begins with traditional materials — references to the Seven Sages, and then to Pythagoras, the first to call himself not a wise man but a wisdom-lover. Today, when we call to mind the literal meaning of Philosophia — love of wisdom — we realize it has dwindled into a dead metaphor. Yet Dante experienced that Love and that Wisdom as if on the first day of creation. For him Wisdom was alive, and Love was her form, her soul,[37] and he celebrated her with a freshness and a passion that challenges not just our willingness but our capacity to suspend disbelief.

At one point (viii, 14) Dante tells that Filosofia's loving beauty surpasses our intellect and our gaze, because there the human soul inebriates itself and reels away. It is not easy for us, who can readily locate in a good academic library most of the works to which Dante had access, to fathom how intoxicating his discovery of these for himself must have been: he, a layman, finding first Boethius' *Consolation* and Cicero's *On Friendship*, and then an eclectic but wide range of texts, from the lyrical exaltation of Sapientia in the Solomonic books to the lapidary sentences of the *Liber de causis*; to the sheer intellectual magnitude and breadth of Aristotle and his commentators, Moslem and Christian; to the scientific works — of Alfraganus, Alpetragius, Alhazen — that still had scarcely passed beyond the confines of a small clerical avant-garde. The penetrating of such a panoply of texts by one who had not come to them through a lifelong

[34] *Conv.* III, xiv, 15.

[35] I have discussed these two tributes in some detail on two occasions: in the essay 'Orizzonte che rischiari', *The Medieval Poet and his World* (Rome, 1984), pp. 407-30, and in the section 'Boethius and Siger' in *Dante and Medieval Latin Traditions* (Cambridge, 1986), pp. 96-100, 143-44 n. 51.

[36] *Conv.* III, xi, 3 ff.

[37] *Conv.* III, xiii, 10: *amore è forma di Filosofia, e però qui si chiama anima di lei.*

career in the schools must have carried with it something of that sense of risk and adventure of the mind which in a later period would be called Faustian.

Dante insists that the bond between the Wisdom-lover and his beloved must be mutual. He exploits a lovely ambiguity in the term *studio*: it is at the same time study and pursuit — the eager pursuit of love — 'when on one side love is already born, and one longs and strives for it to be on the other person's side too'.[38] In describing this mutual love, Dante uses Cicero's and Aristotle's characterizations of perfect friendship: this is a relation that goes beyond pleasure and beyond advantage (though there are many, Dante admits, who study for motives such as these). No, it is a bond between two persons purely for its own sake, utterly disinterested.

Again we see what I would call not a contamination but an alchemy of sources: as his *auctoritas* for this Aristotelian-Ciceronian conception of truly mutual friendship, Dante cites Sapientia from the Book of Proverbs: 'I love those who love me'.[39] And soon we perceive that underlying the whole allegorical fiction here is not a Graeco-Roman ideal of friendship but rather Solomon's relation to Sapientia — an imagined love between a man and a woman. The Aristotelian pursuit of wisdom is transformed into a sublime love-relationship. We begin to understand why Filosofia, in these pages and in the verses they expound, becomes so much more than a personified discipline or way of life.

Dante alludes to and cites from the Sapiential passages in Proverbs, Wisdom, and Ecclesiasticus; when he cites the Song of Songs, he is fully alive to the allegorization of Solomon's 'bride, sister and beloved' as Sapientia.

Sapientia in the Solomonic books is both an earthly condition of felicity and a transcendent being, the beautiful and creative divine companion. In Proverbs, on the one hand: 'My fruit is better than gold and precious stone, my products better than choice silver . . . I shall walk on the ways of justice . . . to enrich those who love me' (8, 19-21). On the other: 'The Lord possessed me as the beginning of his ways . . . I was established eternally . . .[40] There were not yet abysses and I was already conceived . . . When he prepared the heavens I was there . . . when he hung the foundations of the earth I was with him, harmonizing all things, and I took delight each day, playing in his presence at all times, playing throughout the universe; and my delight was to be with the sons of men' (8, 22-31). In the Book of Wisdom, similarly, Solomon says of the felicity Sapientia can bestow: 'I set her above kingdoms and thrones, and held riches as naught compared with her . . . I loved her beyond health and beauty, and resolved to have her as my light, for

[38] *Conv.* III, xii, 3-4.

[39] *Conv.* III, xi, 12.

[40] In his critical edition, *Biblia Sacra iuxta Vulgatam versionem* (2nd ed., 2 vols., Stuttgart, 1975), Robert Weber follows the MSS that here read: *Dominus possedit me initium viarum suarum . . . ab aeterno ordita sum*. This corresponds to the Greek of the Septuagint; but the readings *initio*/*in initio* and *ordinata* are also well attested in early MSS. From *Amor che nella mente* v. 54 (*però fu tal da etterno ordinata*) it would seem that Dante knew this verse at least with the reading *ordinata*.

her brightness is inextinguishable. But all good things came to me together with her, and endless honour at her hands, and I rejoiced in all things' (7, 8-12). Those who make use of her treasure 'become sharers of the friendship of God' (7, 14). At the same time, Sapientia is again of cosmic stature: 'the pure emanation of the radiance of the almighty God . . . the untarnished mirror of God's majesty and image of his bounty. And though she is one, she is capable of all, and abiding in herself she makes all things new' (7, 25-27).[41]

Yet even when she is seen as a divine emanation, Sapientia can be the speaker's own heavenly beloved: 'I have loved her and pursued her since my youth, and strove to take her as my bride; I was in love with her beauty . . . so I resolved to bring her to share my life' (8, 2-9). In his prayer to God, Solomon bridges the transcendent and terrestrial images of Wisdom: 'Send her from your holy heavens, and from the throne of your greatness, that she may be with me and may work with me, that I may know what is pleasing to you' (9, 10).

In Ecclesiasticus, as in Proverbs, Sapientia declares herself: 'I came forth from the mouth of the highest one, the first-born daughter, before every creature. I made an unfailing brightness rise in the heavens, and covered all the earth as with a mist . . . I have dwelt in every land and every people . . . I was created in the beginning, before the ages, and shall not pass away in the age to come . . . Come to me, all you who long for me, and take your fill of what I bring forth: for my spirit is sweeter than honey . . . and I shall make intoxicating the fruit of my field' (24, 5-42).

In these brief quotations I have not entirely confined myself to phrases cited or adapted by Dante in his canzone or his commentary, but have tried to signal a few of the moments which we can perceive had particular imaginative resonance for him. I have not yet touched on the fourth Solomonic text, the Song of Songs, which goes beyond such terms as divine possession, emanation, mirror or first-born, such as we know from the Sapiential books, to the beloved as bride, *sponsa*. It is this that Dante dwells on above all at the rapturous climax of his twelfth chapter, in which the Donna Gentile is seen as an aspect of the divine essence. For, when God contemplates Wisdom, he is contemplating his own essence. Thus, says Dante,

> she is most noble, because the divine essence is most noble; and she exists in God in a perfect and true fashion, as it were through an eternal marriage. In the other Intelligences she exists in a lesser fashion, as it were like a mistress in whom no lover can take complete joy, but contents his longing by looking at her . . . Oh noblest and most excellent heart, that strives for fulfilment in the bride of the Emperor of heaven — and not only bride but sister and most beloved daughter![42]

[41] With the last phrase, compare esp. *Conv.* III, viii, 20: *la sua bellezza ha podestade in rinnovare natura in coloro che la mirano; ch'è miracolosa cosa.*

[42] *Conv.* III, xii, 13-14: 'ed è nobilissima, però che nobilissima è la essenzia divina; ed è in lui per modo perfetto e vero, quasi per etterno matrimonio. Ne l'altre intelligenze è per modo minore, quasi

The bride is called sister — *soror* — as she often is in the Song of Songs, and daughter, like the divine *primogenita* of Ecclesiasticus. But Dante adds a sexual element to the language, comparable to that in the Book of Wisdom,[43] yet distinct from it and more daring: the Donna Gentile is both bride and mistress, *sposa* and *druda*. This conjunction, I would suggest, owes at least a little to that in the Book of Proverbs, just cited, where Sapientia takes delight each day playing in the presence of the Creator, but her delight is also to be with the sons of men. Yet this contrast is fused in Dante's imagination with a marvellous passage in Aristotle's *Metaphysics*, where wisdom, the 'first philosophy', is called 'most divine and most to be reverenced . . . goddess of the sciences: such a knowledge will be the only one that is called divine, for two reasons: because it is possessed most of all by God, and because it is about things divine'.[44] And, perhaps even more surprisingly, Dante has a high Scholastic authority for his image of the *druda*: in his commentary on the discussion of friendship in Aristotle's *Ethics*, Thomas Aquinas explains that 'living together (*convictus*) is grounded in a certain assimilation of friendship to lustful love, where we see especially that the thing lovers desire above all is to look at the women they love . . . for it is through sight most of all that the passion of love arises and is maintained. Such love is aroused particularly by the beauty perceived through sight'.[45]

The *druda* passage is only one of several where Dante allows his Sapiential language to become open to erotic connotations. Thus for instance, just before citing Sapientia's words 'I love those who love me' (xi, 12), he tells that 'the true philosopher loves each part of Wisdom, and Wisdom loves each part of the philosopher, in that she draws him totally to herself and lets no thought of his stray elsewhere'. Or again, three chapters later: 'the sight of this lady was so generously ordained for us — not just to see her face, which she shows us, but to long to win what she keeps hidden' (xiv, 13).

At the same time, Dante is able to play upon the most solemn biblical connotations: when he cites Wisdom's words from Ecclesiasticus — 'I was created from the beginning before the ages . . .' and from Proverbs — 'I was established eternally' — Dante adds: 'and at the opening of John's Gospel one can plainly note her eternity'.[46] His reference is clearly to *hoc erat in principio*

come druda de la quale nullo amadore prende compiuta gioia, ma nel suo aspetto contentan la loro vaghezza . . . Oh nobilissimo ed eccellentissimo cuore, che ne la sposa de lo Imperadore del cielo s'intende, e non solamente sposa, ma suora e figlia dilettissima!'.

[43] Cf. especially Wisdom 8, 16:

Going into my house, I shall sleep with her,
for her company has no bitterness,
living with her has no weariness,
but joy and bliss.

[44] *Metaph.* I, 2, 983a, 4-10, in the Latin transl. cit. Vasoli, p. 441.

[45] *Exp. Eth.* IX, lect. xiv, 1944, cit. Vasoli, p. 443.

[46] *Conv.* III, xiv, 7.

apud Deum: the Logos 'was in the beginning with God'. Yet I am not altogether happy with Vasoli's comment: 'Here Dante's identification of Filosofia or Sapienza with the Verbum Dei is evident'.[47] For Dante explicitly calls the Donna Gentile *creatura* (viii, 3); and in the Solomonic texts too, Sapientia, though eternal, always affirms herself as created. She is God's *primogenita*, created from the beginning, she is called his emanation, his companion, even his bride. By contrast, the Logos, the Word made flesh, was not created.

More precisely, I would say that Dante here shows his awareness of a long tradition, prevalent from late Antiquity onwards, of identifying the feminine Sophia/Sapientia with the masculine Logos — a tradition that has been admirably documented and analysed in a group of essays by Marie-Thérèse d'Alverny.[48] Yet this tradition, that tends to make such an identification, naturally also forfeits all the connotations of the womanly beloved, the bride in the primordial mystic love-union. And Dante was determined not to forfeit these. Hence, even in his swift allusion to the prologue of John at this moment, he has the artistic tact not to dwell on the merging of Sophia and Logos in such a way as would break the spell of his metaphorics of the heavenly beloved.

The closest that Dante comes to a full divinization of Sapientia is perhaps in his verse *Costei pensò chi mosse l'universo* ('She was the thought of him who moved the universe'): if God, the unmoved mover, contemplates her when he contemplates his essence, then, as Dante makes explicit, 'she is the divine philosophy of the divine essence' (xii, 13); but God comprehends a multitude of forms in his mind, and all of these, as contemplated by God, are aspects of the divine essence. Filosofia is God's thought; Dante does not say she is God's Word.

Yet there is still another allusion that seems to go in this direction in the final chapter of *Convivio* III, as Dante reaches the culmination of his praises of Wisdom: 'I say she is the mother of all and prior to every principle, saying that with her God began the world and especially the motion of the firmament . . .' After citing four verses from Sapientia's proclamation of herself in Proverbs — 'When he prepared the heavens I was there . . .' — Dante ends with the impassioned cry:

> Oh you, worse than dead, who flee from her friendship, open your eyes and see: for before you existed she was your lover, preparing and ordering your unfolding; and when you were made, she came to you in your likeness, so as to guide you![49]

[47] Vasoli, p. 458.

[48] *Études sur le symbolisme de la Sagesse et sur l'iconographie* (Aldershot, 1992). While, as I briefly indicated in my Preface to this volume (p. x), one may have some reservations about method in the essay 'Dante et la Sagesse' (Ch. IV), this in no way applies to the other 'Sapiential' essays collected there. The most pertinent to the Sophia/Logos question is the succinct, penetrating piece, 'Le symbolisme de la Sagesse et le Christ de Saint Dunstan' (Ch. II).

[49] *Conv.* III, xv, 15-17.

Once more Dante shows himself aware of the possible Christological associations — the Word incarnate, according to the likeness of men (*in similitudinem hominum*)[50] — yet again he does not allow these associations to result in a fusion of Sophia and Logos, or to warp the texture of his allegorical fiction. She remains the Donna Gentile, the miracle who is visible every day, whose human beauty even the most stolid or corrupt or avaricious Florentine could behold and cherish, if only he wished. It is significant that in the sentence immediately after 'she came to you in your likeness', Dante, enhancing the feminine associations, calls her 'this eternal Empress'. Dante's genius is fleetingly to evoke the Logos connotation but not to let it dominate — to make it functionally wholly subordinate to the celebration of the Donna Gentile. Dante's artistic ideal of functionality is such that, in an aside earlier in the third treatise, he had said: 'That utterance comes from the rhetorician's workshop, in which each part sets its hand to the principal intent' (iv, 3).[51] And it is not to belittle Dante's two Logos-allusions to say that they set their hands to his principal intent: the exaltation of the womanly beloved.

The pursuit of wisdom — the love of the Donna Gentile — leads to beatitude or felicity (Dante uses *beatitudine* and *felicitade* synonymously, as Boethius had used *beatitudo* and *felicitas*). How far is the loving union with this Donna attainable by human beings in their earthly existence? And how far is the desire bound to remain incompletely satisfied this side of heaven? The third treatise of the *Convivio* gives conflicting indications. There is nothing as clear-cut as the famous passage near the close of the *Monarchia*, in which Dante was to affirm that divine Providence 'set humanity two goals (*duos fines*) to pursue: the felicity of this life, which consists in the unfolding of one's own capacities, and which is figured by the earthly paradise; and the felicity of eternal life, which consists in enjoying the sight of God, towards which one's own capacities cannot ascend unless helped by divine light, which is signified by the celestial paradise'.[52] By the time Dante wrote the *Monarchia*, that is, he had decisively separated two distinct ultimate felicities — *duo ultima* — even if, in the tantalizing final phrases of that work, he still concedes that 'this mortal felicity is in some way (*quodam modo*) ordered towards immortal felicity'.[53] This would imply that the Aristotelian goal of a mortal felicity, achieved through contemplation, through which, Aristotle believed, human beings can become as divine as possible, was not quite self-sufficient after all.

And it is precisely such an ambiguity, such a hesitance, that we can observe more fully in *Convivio* III. There Dante's divergences of emphasis have led to much controversy in our century. In brief: did Dante at this stage of his thought

[50] Philippians 2, 7.
[51] I have discussed the notion of functionality in the writings of medieval rhetoricians in an essay, 'Medieval Rhetoric', in *The Medieval Poet and his World* (cit. n. 35), pp. 7-38.
[52] *Monarchia*, III, xvi, 7.
[53] Ibid. 17.

uphold a purely rational goal of human fulfilment? Did he reckon with a Christian conception of the beatific vision, distinct from the love of the Donna Gentile? Or did he blend the two conceptions, absorbing the religious goal into the rational? It is possible to retrace, or at least swiftly indicate, some of the windings of Dante's thought on this topic, without wishing (as many scholars have done) either to claim him for perfect Christian orthodoxy, or to condemn — or else praise — him for his apparent departures from such orthodoxy.

By the time he wrote the *Convivio*, Dante was familiar with a range of philosophical images that tended in diverse directions. The *Liber de causis*, for instance, suggested an emanationist world-picture: there, as we saw, the divine *discorrimento* descends from the first cause, the *summum bonum*, by way of the Intelligences to the sublunary world. It was easy for Dante to give the Donna Gentile a specific rôle in that process of mediation: the Intelligences know her in the divine mind (*Ogni Intelletto di là su la mira*), and she is the specific mediatrix of their knowledge to human beings.

Yet, through the radical Latin Aristotelians, or Averroists, of his own day, Dante was familiar too with a different notion of the *summum bonum*: for them it was something attainable by human contemplation alone, through which humans arrive at what Dante calls *deitade*, even in their life on earth. In a brief treatise by Boethius of Dacia (i.e. of Denmark), which revealingly has not only the title 'The supreme good' (*De summo bono*), but in the earliest complete manuscript is headed 'The philosopher's life' (*Vita philosophi*),[54] the Aristotelian notion of contemplation as the truly human goal is celebrated with mystical fervour.[55]

Dante in the *Convivio* attempted to make these perspectives complementary rather than contradictory. For him, we might say, the downward *discorrimento*, of which the mental model lies in the emanations evoked in the *Liber de causis*, is completed by an upward surge of human contemplation, where the mental model lies in some of the highest moments of Latin Aristotelianism, such as the climax of Boethius of Dacia's discourse: The philosopher, 'living according to the right order of nature, has acquired the best and ultimate goal of human life'.[56]

At the same time, when — as he tells us — Dante, in love with the Donna Gentile, sought her 'in the schools of the religious and the disputations of the philosophers' (II, xii, 7), at least in the schools of the religious, at Santa Croce or Santa Maria Novella, he will have met a conception of heavenly felicity that was in no sense reducible to Aristotelian contemplation.

At the first mention of this problematic in *Convivio* III, the convictions of the schools of the religious dominate Dante's thought. The desire for perfection, he says (vi, 7), is 'the desire that always makes every delight seem defective to us —

[54] Ed. N. J. Green-Pedersen, in *Boethii Daci Opera*, VI, 2: *Opuscula* (Corpus Philosophorum Danicorum Medii Aevi, Copenhagen, 1976), pp. 367-77. On the manuscripts cf. ibid. pp. xxiv-xlii.

[55] In his treatise Boethius of Dacia does not reject the notion that faith promises a different beatitude in a future life, but leaves this at the margin of his exposition. Cf. also p. 51 below.

[56] *De summo bono*, p. 377, lines 241-42.

for no delight in this life is so great that it can take away the thirst from our soul'. This, as Vasoli aptly notes, seems to be a paraphrase of a passage in Thomas Aquinas's *Contra Gentiles*;[57] Dante will likewise have recalled Augustine's ardent address to God at the opening of the *Confessions*: 'our heart is restless till it rests in you'.[58]

Two chapters later, discussing the verses

> Cose appariscon ne lo suo aspetto,
> che mostran de' piacer di paradiso — (55 f.)
>
> In her aspect things appear
> that show some of the joys of paradise —

Dante in his commentary repeats the partitive genitive *de' piacer* ('some of the joys') and adds:

> among the others, the noblest joy, which is the beginning and end of all the rest, is contentment, and this is to attain beatitude (*essere beato* — literally, to be blessed or blissful). And this joy is truly in her aspect, though in a different way . . . for contentment in paradise is perpetual, which this contentment can by no means be.[59]

The joy in contemplating the Donna Gentile, that is, can be truly paradisal even in this life: yet in this life it cannot show the totality of the joys of paradise, nor their everlastingness. Through love of Wisdom we can already know the quality of the ultimate felicity, but not its fullness. Here 'paradise' refers unmistakably to the celestial paradise, conceived as the one-and-only ultimate goal. Dante has not yet arrived at his conception of the *two* ultimates, one of which, figured in the earthly paradise, bodies forth an ultimate earthly goal of felicity.

There is a further brief allusion that is relevant, but in a passage where the text remains at one point not fully certain. Love, Dante reminds us (xiii, 10-11), is the form of Filosofia, and therefore it is here called her soul. 'This love is manifest in the exercise of Wisdom (*ne l'uso de la Sapienza*), which brings with it (*lo quale seco conduce*)[60] wondrous beauties — that is, contentment in every condition of time, and scorn for those things which others make into their lords'. The

[57] Cited above, n. 29.

[58] *Conf.* I, i, 1: *inquietum est cor nostrum donec requiescat in te.*

[59] *Conv.* III, viii, 5.

[60] Once more I believe Simonelli's analysis (*Materiali*, cit. n. 21, p. 225) is the most convincing: the archetype had *ne l'uso de la Sapienza lo quale esso conduce*; the only change needed, she suggests, is to correct *esso* to *seco*. The MS reading *uso* should not be changed, as Nardi emphasized, since it is confirmed by *uso* in III, xii, 12 and *usando* in III, xii, 2. Vasoli reports these points in his notes (p. 450), and assents ('Le ipotesi dei due studiosi sembrano, anche a me, accettabili'). Ageno (p. 234) prints 'nel *v*iso della Sapienza, [nel]lo quale essa conduce'. The *a* of *essa* is not italicized; at the same time, there is no indication in her apparatus that *essa* has any MS support.

expression 'contentment in every condition of time' seems to stake a claim beyond that of the moment when Dante had stressed that the paradisal joys, as we can know them on earth, are not perpetual — and there is no explicit allusion at this point to a more complete kind of felicity.

The most detailed discussion of the topic comes in the final chapter of treatise III, in the allegorical exposition of the joys to be found in the Donna Gentile's eyes and smile — Filosofia's demonstrations and persuasions:

in these one experiences that highest joy of felicity (*beatitudine*), which is the greatest good in paradise. This joy cannot exist in anything here below except in contemplating those eyes and that smile . . . In this gaze alone is human perfection acquired, that is, the perfection of reason, on which our entire essence depends as on its most principal part . . .[61]

Aristotle and the Book of Wisdom are adduced as authorities for the affirmation that in wisdom lies felicity and divinity. And yet in the canzone the verses continue, saying of the paradisal joys in the lady's eyes and smile:

> Elle soverchian lo nostro intelletto
> come raggio di sole un frale viso. (59 f.)
>
> They surpass our intellect
> as the sun's ray surpasses a frail gaze.

This brings Dante to the heart of his philosophical problem about felicity:

Truly here someone may seriously wonder how wisdom can make a person blissful (*beato*) if it is unable to show him certain things perfectly — inasmuch as his natural desire is to know, and without fulfilling that desire he cannot be blissful.

To this one can clearly answer that the natural desire in each being is measured according to the capacity of the being which desires, that otherwise would frustrate itself, which is impossible, and Nature would have made it in vain, which is likewise impossible . . .

Thus the human desire is measured in this life to match the knowledge that can be possessed here . . . So, inasmuch as it is impossible for our nature to know what God is, and what certain other beings are, that is not something which we naturally desire to know.[62]

[61] *Conv.* III, xv, 2-4.

[62] *Conv.* III, xv, 7-9:

Veramente può qui alcuno forte dubitare come ciò sia, che la sapienza possa fare l'uomo beato, non potendo a lui perfettamente certe cose mostrare; con ciò sia cosa che 'l naturale desiderio sia a l'uomo di sapere, e sanza compiere lo desiderio beato essere non possa.

A ciò si può chiaramente rispondere che lo desiderio naturale in ciascuna cosa è misurato secondo la possibilitade de la cosa desiderante: altrimenti andrebbe in contrario di sé medesimo, che impossibile è; e la Natura l'avrebbe fatto indarno, che è anche impossibile . . .

In the heavenly realm Dante postulates a similar measuring: in the angels the desire for wisdom is measured to match their diverse capacities for it; the saints feel no envy that other saints may be nearer to God than they: the desire of each is wholly fulfilled, measured to match the goodness of their nature.

Here we have come a long way from Augustine and Aquinas: for Dante, it now seems, there is a felicity, a thirst that *can* be slaked, a craving that can find its rest, *quodam modo* — in some way — even in this life. The desire for the Donna Gentile need not be frustrating and forever unfulfillable: it can be satisfied to the utmost limits of human nature, in accordance with which it is measured — even if, in a paradise beyond that nature, there are things which surpass our understanding.[63]

Dante, still acknowledging an otherworldly felicity incommensurable with the one attainable through contemplation in this life, has moved close to acknowledging the earthly felicity as a goal in its own right — the goal that, in the *Monarchia,* he would embody in the image of the earthly paradise.

His intellectual position in this matter cannot be reduced to any formula. Clearly it is opposed to the position of Thomas Aquinas, for whom true felicity can only be otherworldly. Yet Dante's position is not identical either with that unconditional celebration of contemplative earthly felicity which we find in the tenth book of Aristotle's *Ethics*: Dante's continual allusions to an otherworldly dimension suffice to make this plain. The thinker closest to Dante in outlook, and who probably influenced him most deeply in this question, was one who had succeeded in being a truly committed Aristotelian as well as a truly committed Christian: Albert the Great. The relation between Albert's thought and Dante's has been finely observed, first by Nardi, more recently by Corti and Vasoli. Yet I have a small contribution to add. In Albert's discussion of Book X of the *Ethics* in his greater commentary, *Super Ethica,* certain insights occur that have not yet been noted by the scholars, but which I believe can illuminate Dante's thoughts about felicity and contemplation better than any of the texts so far adduced.

Albert begins his commentary on Book X by citing the opening of Boethius' poem about Orpheus and Eurydice:

> Felix qui potuit boni
> fontem visere lucidum,
> felix qui potuit gravis
> terrae solvere vincula!

> E però l'umano desiderio è misurato in questa vita a quella scienza che qui avere si può . . . Onde, con ciò sia cosa che conoscere di Dio (e di certe altre cose) quello esso è non sia possibile a la nostra natura, quello da noi naturalmente non è desiderato di sapere.

quello esso è: I accept Simonelli's suggestion (cit. Vasoli, p. 485) about keeping the text of the archetype; similarly Ageno, p. 247.

[63] Already Boethius, at his first sight of Philosophia, had perceived precisely the paradox of her ambiguous stature: see the passage from *The Consolation of Philosophy*, I pr. 1, translated below, p. 75.

Blissful he who could behold
the lucent fountain of the good;
blissful he who could shake off
the shackles of the heavy earth!

Albert sees these verses as epitomizing the whole substance of Aristotle's tenth book:

for the good is above all what is good in itself, to which other things are ordered, and this is especially the perfect activity of the speculative intellect, which is called contemplative felicity. Its fountain is the divine intellect, which gushes forth the light of cognition into all things that know; contemplative felicity exists through imitation of that fountain, for the ultimate perfection of all our contemplation lies in him who is the most longed-for object of knowledge . . .

But God contemplates his own intellect most perfectly, and by understanding himself understands all other things. And so contemplative felicity is a kind of imitation of the divine intellect . . .[64]

And yet, is not imitation doomed to remain forever short of perfection? The divine intellect surpasses the human, no aspiration to be like it can ever be perfectly satisfied. So Albert is led to asking the question that Dante asks in the last chapter of *Convivio* III: can contemplation be, as Aristotle affirms, the supreme human felicity, *delectabilissima*? How can it, since we can never enjoy it completely? —

For where what gives delight is not perfectly conjoined [to the contemplator], it cannot be a perfect delight; but things divine are not perfectly conjoined to us, because we do not comprehend them fully.[65]

Albert's answer comes close to Dante, and may indeed have inspired Dante's thoughts about what is measured to the capacity of each knower:

To this first point, then, it should be said that, although things divine are not perfectly conjoined to us in their own mode, *they are nonetheless perfectly conjoined to us*

[64] Boethius, ibid. III m. 12, 1-4; Albertus Magnus, *Super Ethica Commentum et Quaestiones* (= *Opera Omnia*, XIV, 2), ed. Wilhelmus Kübel (Münster i. W., 1987), p. 708a, 12-25: 'bonum enim maxime est illud quod per se bonum est et ad quod alia ordinantur, et hoc praecipue est perfecta operatio intellectus speculativi, quae dicitur felicitas contemplativa. Huius autem fons est divinus intellectus, qui profundit lumen cognitionis in omnia cognoscentia et per cuius imitationem est felicitas contemplativa, quia perfectio ultima omnis nostrae contemplationis est in eo qui est maxime desideratum ad sciendum . . . ipse autem deus intellectum suum perfectissime contemplatur, et intelligendo se intelligit omnia alia. Et ideo contemplativa felicitas est quaedam imitatio divini intellectus . . .'.

[65] Ibid. p. 752a, 41-44: 'Ubi enim illud quod delectat non perfecte coniungitur, non potest esse perfecta delectatio; sed divina non perfecte coniunguntur nobis, quia non plene comprehendimus ipsa'.

according to the measure of our disposition, whether this disposition is acquired or infused; and in accordance with this they are fitting for us.[66]

Contemplation, however, does not always bring felicity. There can be a failure, emotional or intellectual, on the contemplator's part. We have not yet turned to the final strophe, the envoi or *congedo*, of *Amor che nella mente*, in which Dante alludes to a temporary failure in his own contemplation, and analyses the reasons for it.

He notes that, whilst in this canzone he has praised the Donna Gentile as an 'exemplar of humility' (*essemplo d'umiltate*), in a sister-song he had called her 'fierce and disdainful' (*fera e disdegnosa*). The sister-song, the ballata *Voi che savete*,[67] which is not in the *Convivio*, had, Dante now claims, been a delusion, a failure of vision, such as when we see the sky — which in itself is always luminous and clear — as darkened, affirming that the stars are dimmed. Dante bids his new song, *Amor che nella mente*, to make its excuses to the Donna Gentile — and yet, as Foster-Boyde subtly observed,[68] it is really the earlier, deluded song, *Voi che savete*, which is being excused.

The excuses for this ballata are made at length in the ninth and tenth chapters of *Convivio* III. The allusion to visual impairment in his canzone leads Dante to a learned excursus on the nature of vision, with references to Plato and no fewer than three works of Aristotle's. Then Chapter x begins, 'Leaving this digression, which was necessary in order to see the truth . . .' There is a captivating faux-naïf quality in the way Dante introduces such digressions, solemnly bringing on a brigade of philosophical arguments and authorities to support a simple human point. In just this way in Chapter iv he had brought on Aristotle's *Ethics* to explain the nature of excusing, and in Chapter v had given a long and brilliant astronomical exposition, invoking Aristotle, Albert the Great, and even the poet Lucan, ostensibly because this was necessary in order to understand perfectly the song's quite straightforward phrase, 'the sun, that circles the whole world' (*il sol, che tutto 'l mondo gira*). When at last Dante begins the next chapter affirming that, since the mode in which the sun revolves has been shown, 'one can now proceed to demonstrate the meaning' of this part of the canzone, he is adroitly making us accomplices in his intellectual gambit. The excursus in Chapter ix is no more necessary to Dante's poetic argument than that in Chapter v: Dante knows it, and knows that we know.

Yet there is also something more serious underlying both the ballata and the excuses made for it — obliquely — in the *Convivio*, which deserves closer

[66] Ibid. p. 753a, 14-19 (italics mine): 'Ad primum ergo dicendum, quod quamvis non perfecte coniungantur nobis divina secundum modum ipsorum, *coniunguntur tamen perfecte secundum mensuram habitus nostri* sive acquisiti sive infusi, et secundum hoc etiam sunt nobis convenientia'.
[67] Foster-Boyde no. 60 (I, 104).
[68] Ibid. II, 183.

attention. In *Voi che savete*, the lady is cruel and scornful, nonetheless Love is in her eyes:

Par ch'ella dica: 'Io non sarò umile
verso d'alcun che ne li occhi mi guardi,
ch'io ci porto entro quel segnor gentile
che m'ha fatto sentir de li suoi dardi'.

She seems to say: 'I shall not be gentle
to anyone who looks into my eyes,
for in them I bear that noble lord
who made me feel his shafts'.

She declares she will not be gentle, that is, because she has herself been wounded by Love. If we think of the speaker here as Filosofia — and the allusions to this ballata in the *Convivio* oblige us to do so — the imagined situation must be something like this. She *has* felt love for some who have wooed her, and then been disappointed in them — just as Boethius' Philosophia had found that so many of her suitors turned out to be unworthy and base. So instead this lady, like Prudentia in the traditional iconography of the cardinal Virtues,[69] retreats into contemplating herself —

per vederli per sé quando le piace,
a quella guisa retta donna face
quando si mira per volere onore.

to see her eyes for herself, when it pleases her,
in the way a virtuous lady does
when she gazes at herself for honour's sake.

Filosofia, that is, finding perfect fulfilment in her own contemplation, need make no concessions to the inadequate lovers who still hope for the answering light of love in her eyes.

What is astonishing in a song whose language had been moving wholly in the expressive sphere of the *dolce stil nuovo* is the vehemence of Dante's conclusion:

Ma quanto vuol nasconda e guardi lui,
ch'io non veggia talor tanta salute;
però che i miei disiri avran vertute
contra 'l disdegno che mi dà tremore.

But let her hide and keep back Love as much as she please,
to prevent my ever seeing such salvation —
for my desires shall nonetheless prevail

[69] Cf. Gianfranco Contini, *Rime* (cit. Ch. I n. 1), p. 380.

> against the scorn that causes me to tremble.

It is as if Dante were carrying over into his allegory something of the passionate violence, the fantasy of winning love by force, that he evoked erotically in another canzone, *Così nel mio parlar.*[70]

The prose exegesis accords well with this. Dante claims that he now sees that his perception of this lady 'discorded from the truth because of a sickness of the soul, which was impassioned by too much desire'.[71] If at the end of the third treatise Dante briefly translates this into allegorical terms — the Donna Gentile seemed to look at him fiercely because he couldn't yet understand her persuasive words, and seemed disdainful because he did not grasp her demonstrations[72] — the language in the literal exposition is more and more suggestive of a sensual defect. Dante explains in Aristotelian terms that the closer the desired being comes to the desirer, 'the greater is the longing, and the soul, more passionate, unites itself the more with the concupiscent part, abandoning reason all the more, so that then it judges the person not like a human being, but almost like another animal, only according to appearance, not discerning the truth'.[73]

Notwithstanding Dante's invoking of Aristotle here as his *auctoritas*, this does not sound like a purely philosophical flaw. The semblance of scorn and ferocity in this lady — whose countenance, Dante insists, was in truth full of honour — seems to have been caused 'by too much desire', and it would be hard to give this expression a solely philosophical, and not emotional, meaning. This is borne out by a small detail in the last strophe of *Amor che nella mente* — a detail on which I have seen no discussion by commentators. After speaking of his excessive desire, Dante explains the phrase in the canzone that begins *ché l'anima temea* . . . ('for my soul was afraid . . .'), with the words 'so that whatever I saw in her presence seemed fierce to me'. But he does not comment, either literally or allegorically, on the continuation of this phrase, with its remarkable present tenses:

> ché l'anima temea,
> *e teme ancora*, sì che mi par fero
> quantunqu'io veggio là 'v' ella mi senta.
>
> for my soul was afraid,
> *and is still afraid*, so that whatever I see
> when she looks at me, seems to me fierce.

[70] Foster-Boyde no. 80 (esp. st. 6, I, 174).
[71] *Conv.* III, x, 1.
[72] *Conv.* III, xv, 19.
[73] *Conv.* III, x, 2. Dante here alludes to 'the Philosopher in his book *De generatione*'; but for the complex question of the exact passages in Aristotle and his Scholastic commentators which were in Dante's mind when he wrote these lines, see Vasoli's notes, pp. 413 f.

The words that are never commented — *e teme ancora* — perhaps needed no comment: they told in all simplicity that the pangs of too great a desire, or of a misdirected desire, could affect Dante still.

To conclude, I should like to explain why I chose the second half of my title for this chapter. When, in the sixth book of the *Aeneid*, the Sibyl, possessed by the god Apollo, foretells Aeneas's destiny, Vergil says she was 'wrapping truth in dark sayings' — *obscuris vera involvens* (VI, 100). In the early twelfth century, the poet-philosopher Bernardus Silvestris twice discussed the meaning of Vergil's words. Introducing his commentary on Martianus Capella's fantasy *The Marriage of Philology and Mercury* with an account of the nature and functions of hidden meanings, he glosses *obscuris vera involvens* as *divina integumentis claudens*:[74] the Sibyl, that is, was enclosing divine content, or things divine, in *integumenta* — in poetic, fictive or mythological coverings, such as a wise commentator can uncover, so as to reveal the divine meaning beneath.

In his *Aeneid* commentary (which it is possible, though not certain, that Dante knew directly),[75] Bernardus stresses that the Sibyl was also *hiding* the truth by way of her *integumenta* — *Veritatem per integumenta occultat* — so that the profane should not find her meaning and mock.[76] However much the commentator may elucidate, the poet can, like the Sibyl, make his *obscura* deliberately dark. Thus, says Bernardus, Martianus, in revealing the deification of human nature by way of his allegory, 'expresses nothing without some mystery'. Thereby he 'speaks as a prudent theologian should'.[77]

Dante, in his evocation of the Donna Gentile, seems to me both like the Sibyl, wrapping truth in dark sayings, and like the commentator Bernardus, uncovering the things divine hidden therein, while also knowing, again like Bernardus, that there are some meanings it is prudent not to uncover too much. Yet it may be possible to see still a further sense (not a Vergilian one) in which Dante is

[74] I have translated the passage in full, with detailed discussion, in *Fabula* (cit. Ch. I n. 3), pp. 119 ff. The work has meanwhile received a complete ed. by H. J. Westra, *The Commentary on Martianus Capella's De nuptiis Philologiae et Mercurii attributed to Bernardus Silvestris* (Toronto, 1986).

[75] Ed. J. W. Jones, E. F. Jones, *The Commentary on the First Six Books of the Aeneid Commonly Attributed to Bernardus Silvestris* (Lincoln-London, 1977). On the question of the (sometimes disputed) ascription to Bernardus of this commentary — and of the Martianus one, whose author cites it as his own earlier work — see esp. my discussion in *Enciclopedia Virgiliana*, I (Rome, 1985), 497-500, s.v. 'Bernardo Silvestre'; Édouard Jeauneau, 'Berkeley, University of California, Bancroft Library MS 2 (Notes de lecture)', *Mediaeval Studies*, 50 (1988), 438-56, at pp. 448-55.

The question of Dante's access to this Vergilian commentary remains delicate (cf. 'Bernardo Silvestre', p. 500). Notwithstanding the categorical claims that it was known to Dante made by Curtius (*European Literature*, cit. Ch. I n. 45, pp. 354 f., = *Europäische Literatur* p. 359) and recently by Maria Corti (*Percorsi dell'invenzione*, Turin, 1993, p. 136), I incline to the more cautious view of Giorgio Padoan, 'Bernardo Silvestre da Tours', *Enciclopedia Dantesca*, I (Rome, 1970), pp. 201-07, and of H. T. Silverstein, whose article 'Dante and Vergil the Mystic', *Harvard Studies and Notes*, 14 (1932), 51-82, though dated in its information concerning Bernardus, remains fundamental for its formulation of the problems and its sensitive analysis of how medieval allegorical reading of Vergil influenced Dante.

[76] *The Commentary*, pp. 50 f.

[77] Ed. Westra (cit. n. 74), p. 46.

obscuris vera involvens. He involves things true with things obscure — he involves truths of philosophy with his own mysteries, the *obscura* of his personal and intellectual development.

III

'ETHICS AND AESTHETICS ARE ONE'

Let me begin by reverting to a text to which I alluded briefly in the last chapter: the treatise, known both as 'The supreme good' and as 'The philosopher's life', which the brilliant Latin Averroist, Boethius of Dacia, wrote around the time of Dante's birth.[1] Among the Dacian's central tenets we can find the following. —

There is a supreme good (*summum bonum*) possible in every species of being. The human one is achieved in accordance with reason and intellect, not with those powers of the soul — sensation and growth — that humans share with beasts or plants. It is achieved both in contemplation and in action.

The intellect is the divine element in the human being, and the supreme human good, in accordance with the intellect's speculative power, is the cognition of truth and the delight in it, this delight being the greater, the nobler the object of the cognition. The *summum bonum*, in accordance with the intellect's practical power, is the achieving of goodness and the delight in that.

This twofold goal is human felicity, the greatest gift we can receive from God in this life; and one who is closer to perfection in this felicity is closer to the felicity that we expect, through faith, in a future life. Yet only the fewest human beings attain such felicity in their earthly existence, because their desires are disordered. It is philosophers, who devote their lives to the pursuit of wisdom, who live as human beings were born to live, for the delectable contemplation of the truth. It is for the sake of this supreme power that all others (including the highest powers of the active life) exist.

These thoughts of Boethius of Dacia seem to me an ideal backdrop against which to look at the arguments that enter the scene and play leading parts in the fourth treatise of Dante's *Convivio*. After the fervent celebration of the Donna Gentile in the third, Dante turns to consider what nobility — her nobility — means in human terms. In an account whose premises, to the best of my knowledge, are very much Dante's own, he presents nobility first as the source and cause of all human virtues, and then as the seed of felicity implanted by God in human souls. Dante's reduction of the many virtues named by Aristotle to a single fount, nobility, and his conjunction of the ethical concept felicity with the theological one of divinely infused grace, are as new, and must have been as unforeseeable to his contemporaries, as was his earlier conjunction of Aristotelian contemplation with love-union to the Donna Gentile, the bride of the Emperor of heaven.[2]

[1] Cf. Green-Pedersen (ed. cit. Ch. II n. 54), pp. xlvii f., though the indications discussed there do not permit a decisive dating.

[2] *Conv.* III, xii, 14.

And yet, throughout the fourth treatise, the links with Latin Averroist thought also remain visible. Dante, like Boethius of Dacia, sees a supreme good, or perfection, attainable in every kind of being — and it is this that he calls its nobility.[3] For him there is likewise a twofold human way, active and contemplative, which leads to the burgeoning of the seed, felicity. For him too it is the contemplative way, the philosophers' way, that attains the most complete felicity of all. And again like his older, Averroist contemporary, however ardently he champions the Aristotelian goal of fulfilment in speculative felicity, he also knows as a Christian that this fulfilment is realizable in its totality not in the present life but only in another. The themes Dante had developed so subtly in his discussion of the felicity of contemplation in treatise III are taken further in IV by considering the effects of that felicity, the moral and intellectual virtues through which the human *summum bonum* can be recognized and defined. But all the essential underlying conceptions, I believe, remain unchanged.

In suggesting this, I am aware that an influential current in recent Dante scholarship seeks to demarcate the fourth treatise of the *Convivio* sharply from the other three. The most radical claims in this direction have been made by Maria Corti, in her book *La felicità mentale*. For Corti, in *Convivio* IV 'it is precisely as regards the notion of felicity that Dante changes his opinion with respect to III'.[4] In treatise IV, he relies on a different range and emphasis of sources: 'in other words, the preceding system of relevant sources has entered a crisis'.[5] It is 'the unconditional love for Aristotelian human philosophy [that] enters a crisis'.[6] 'All the text-levels in treatise IV show a detachment from what precedes: the ideological level, the thematic, the network of sources, the formal levels (syntactic, stylistic, lexical), all collaborate in a new and different interaction'.[7] In particular, Corti would see a new ascendancy of Thomas Aquinas in *Convivio* IV: 'Of St Thomas there are three explicit citations in the fourth treatise, as against only one in the rest of the *Convivio*'.[8]

This leads Corti to her most astonishing inference. Commenting on the evident links between *Convivio* IV and the *Monarchia*, she sees the *Monarchia*'s famous distinction between mortal and immortal felicity, upon which I touched in the last chapter, as 'maturing precisely in the fourth treatise of the *Convivio* . . . where hierarchy triumphs Thomistically (*dove tomisticamente trionfa la gerarchia*)'.[9] In her more recent book, *Percorsi dell'invenzione*, finally, Corti writes of 'that intellectual crisis to which Dante alludes at the beginning of *Convivio* IV, which establishes a kind of ideological-stylistic caesura between treatises II-III and IV of

[3] *Conv.* IV, xvi, 4-5.
[4] *La felicità mentale* (Turin, 1983), p. 58.
[5] Ibid. p. 67.
[6] Ibid. p. 93.
[7] Ibid. p. 124.
[8] Ibid. p. 132.
[9] Ibid. p. 138.

the *Convivio*, and leads to the "troubled attitude" towards the Donna Gentile, who had been the beloved symbol of Aristotelian philosophy in treatises II and III'.[10]

The *stylistic* divergence of treatise IV, both in its canzone and in the mode in which Dante expounds this in his prose, is palpable, and is signalled programmatically by the poet himself:

> Le dolci rime d'amor ch' i' solia
> cercar ne' miei pensieri,
> convien ch'io lasci; non perch'io non speri
> ad esse ritornare,
> ma perché li atti disdegnosi e feri,
> che ne la donna mia
> sono appariti, m'han chiusa la via
> de l'usato parlare.[11]

> The sweet rhymes of love that I was wont
> to search out in my thoughts
> I must now leave; not that I do not hope
> to go back to them,
> but because the disdainful and fierce bearing,
> which has become apparent
> in my lady, has barred the way
> of my accustomed speech.

The verse, Dante promises, will now be harsh and subtle (*rima aspr' e sottile*): soft musicality must yield before the rigours of argument. And indeed this canzone is not only densely and pungently argued, but, as Nardi pointed out long ago, it has the formal severity of a Scholastic *quaestio disputata*:[12] first come the false definitions of nobility, then the critique of these, then the search for the true definition; this is followed by a discussion of the relation of that definition to the Aristotelian conception of virtue, and finally (as a corollary) by an analysis of its manifestations in the four ages of man.

So too at the outset of the prose exposition Dante affirms the primacy of pure argument. The question he is now treating is humanly and politically so urgent — 'to lead people back to the straight path as regards the proper recognition of true nobility' — that 'it was not appropriate to speak figuratively, but rather to give this medicine in the swiftest way, so that health would come back swiftly; for if that is impaired, it is a course to so hideous a death. Thus there is no need, in expounding this, to unfold any allegory, but only to discuss the literal meaning'.[13]

[10] *Percorsi dell'invenzione* (Turin, 1993), p. 155.
[11] *Conv.* IV, Canzone (= Foster-Boyde no. 69), vv. 1-8.
[12] *Dal 'Convivio' alla 'Commedia'* (Rome, 1960), p. 15.
[13] *Conv.* IV, i, 9-11.

Nonetheless, despite these protestations, Dante unfolds in this fourth treatise two of the most original and audacious sustained allegories to be found in the whole of his poetry and prose: first an allegory concerning the three Maries who seek the buried Christ (to which I shall return in detail), then another based on an episode in Lucan, about Marcia, the wife of Cato, who had been parted from Cato and asks him to take her back.[14] It should also be noted that the reasoning in this fourth treatise, with its array of learned reference and Scholastic wealth of detail, is punctuated, far more often than in the preceding ones, by vehement emotional moments, moments of impassioned outcry. The man filled with his mission to proclaim and defend a true conception of nobility is not only one who is suffering exile, but one who has been wounded to the quick, one who, as he looks around him and sees all his ideals scorned, realizes fully,

> Je suis la plaie et le couteau![15]

Change of style and tone in *Convivio* IV, change of technique and purpose — all these I am happy to agree are in the text. But I am unhappy about Corti's notion that an ideological change went along with these; again, I think Dante's 'intellectual crisis' at this time — if we wish to use such an expression — needs extremely careful definition.

The most bizarre aspect of Corti's discussion of *Convivio* IV is her assertion that here, as at the close of the *Monarchia*, 'hierarchy triumphs Thomistically'. For the one thing that Thomas Aquinas could never have admitted was Dante's conception of the 'two ultimates (*duo ultima*) towards which the human being is ordered',[16] the first of which he sees as an earthly beatitude, figured in the earthly paradise. In Dante's thought this beatitude is virtually autonomous: it can be aspired to in its own right and by its own (philosophical) means, independently of the heavenly. For Thomas, mortal felicity is not just, as Dante puts it, 'in some way' ordered towards the immortal: immortal felicity is its sole *raison d'être*. From the notion of the 'two ultimates' Dante drew political inferences about the relation between temporal and spiritual power, between Empire and Church, which were so far from being a 'Thomistic triumph of hierarchy' that for centuries the Church placed his *Monarchia* on its Index of Prohibited Books!

What of the explicit citations of Thomas Aquinas in the *Convivio*? Let us look at them. At II, xiv, 14 Thomas's commentary on Aristotle's *Ethics* is cited, saying that moral philosophy orders us towards the other sciences. At IV, viii, 1 we learn from the same commentary that 'knowing the order of one thing in relation to another is the act proper to reason'; at IV, xv, 12 we are told that both Cicero[17]

[14] *Conv.* IV, xxii, 14-18; xxviii, 13-19.
[15] Charles Baudelaire, 'L'Héautontimorouménos', *Les Fleurs du Mal*, LXXXIII, st. 6.
[16] *Monarchia*, III, xvi, 6; see above, p. 40.
[17] Cf. *De officiis*, I, vi, 18-19.

and Thomas[18] abominate the vice of thinking that one knows everything. There needs no ghost come from the grave to tell us (or Dante) any of this: these particular citations, in a word, are simple commonplaces. Finally, in his last chapter (*Convivio* IV, xxx, 3), Dante explains his choice of title for his canzone: it is 'Contra-li-erranti' ('Against-those-who-err' — the words, he stresses, form a single unit): the name is drawn from 'the good friar Thomas Aquinas, who gave one of his books, which he wrote to confound all those who stray from our faith, the name *Contra Gentiles*'. The implication is that in just this way the canzone will confound all those who stray from Dante's faith about nobility. It is a sign of Dante's sense of humour, not of his conversion to Thomism.

Clearly Dante's direct quotations of Thomas do not exhaust the question of his debt. There are many subtle analogies, especially with passages in Thomas's commentary on the *Ethics*, which do illuminate moments in the *Convivio* (and later in the *Commedia*),[19] and indicate that Dante had reflected keenly on much that he found there. Yet I would also stress that this indirect presence of the *Ethics* commentary is pervasive in the *Convivio*, and already particularly marked in III,[20] even if it is still more noticeable in IV. To see it as distinctive of IV, on the other hand, would be entirely misleading.

What was the 'intellectual crisis' that Dante underwent before he turned to the question of nobility? Let us begin with his own words:

> Since this lady of mine [the Donna Gentile] changed her sweet looks towards me a little, most of all in the area in which I was gazing and seeking whether the primordial matter of the elements was willed by God — for this reason I withheld a little from frequenting her gaze: as if dwelling in her absence, I began to turn my thoughts to the human error about the matter of nobility. And to flee from idleness, which is most of all this lady's enemy, I resolved to cry out to the people who were taking a bad route, so that they could turn to the right one; and I began a canzone . . .[21]

The philosophical question Dante found so thorny that he abandoned it in order to write about nobility — 'whether the primordial matter of the elements was willed by God' — was both less remote and more complex than we might at first surmise. It had quite a history behind it. Boethius comes to just such a problem in the last section of his *Consolation of Philosophy* — a problem so demanding that Philosophia pursues it at some length, without any pause for 'the sweetness of song'. It is here that she explains to Boethius that God is eternal and the world perpetual. The world has no beginning or end, but neither does it have God's unique kind of eternity, which comprises limitless existence all at once. In

[18] *Contra Gentiles*, I, 5.

[19] Cf. Patrick Boyde, *Perception and Passion in Dante's Comedy* (Cambridge, 1993), esp. pp. 225 f., 260 f., 269 f. I discuss Dante's use of the commentary in *Paradiso* 4 in *Dante and Medieval Latin Traditions* (Cambridge, 1986), pp. 30 f., and nn. 65-69 (pp. 132 f.).

[20] The index to the notes in Vasoli, p. 1070, provides ample documentation for this.

[21] *Conv.* IV, i, 8.

that sense the world is not 'coeternal' with God.[22] In the *Consolation of Philosophy* we are left in no doubt that Boethius thought the Platonic and Aristotelian idea of a world which was 'eternal' in the more limited sense was compatible with the notion of divine creation. So too another widely influential work, the Hermetic *Asclepius*, which, as I suggested, Dante knew either directly or by way of Albert the Great,[23] stated quite simply that *Fuit Deus et Hylê* — there was God and primordial matter. It was this key sentence that some of the leading twelfth-century Latin Platonists cited approvingly and developed in their cosmologies.[24] For them God's creative power revealed itself in the ordering of the pre-existing primordial matter into elements; they did not always, or necessarily, accept that this matter, Hylê, was itself created out of nothing by God. It was among the thirteenth-century Latin Aristotelians, who had direct access to Aristotle's arguments for the eternity of the world, that the problem of the relation between that idea and the Christian concept of creation *ex nihilo* came to seem acute.[25] If Aristotle had proved that primordial matter had no beginning, did this not undermine the authority of Genesis? In the decades before Dante concerned himself with philosophy, the thirteenth-century Boethius, he of Dacia, had written a profound and moving little work, *De aeternitate mundi*,[26] in which he had analysed the difficulties that Aristotle's notion of an eternal cosmos posed for one who wanted to renounce neither objective philosophical research nor Christian faith. To him the problem seemed far more intractable, more anxious, than it ever had to his sixth-century namesake. It was, I believe, something of this intractability and anxiety that Dante too perceived and experienced at a particular moment. And the Donna Gentile shed no light. It was this that made Dante turn from a metaphysical question he was uncertain how to resolve to an ethical one where his certainty was absolute.

Much has been written lately, not only by Corti but also, in a more cautious and nuanced fashion, by Vasoli, about the discontinuities between the fourth treatise of the *Convivio* and the preceding ones. In my view, however, the balance, even after Vasoli, still needs some redressing.[27] In what follows I shall

[22] *Cons. Phil.* V pr. 6, 9-59.

[23] See above, p. 32.

[24] *Asclepius*, 14 (*Corpus Hermeticum*, cit. Ch. II n. 27, II, 313). Cf. Bernardus Silvestris, *Cosmographia* (ed. Dronke, Leiden, 1978), II, xiii, 1: 'There were, then, two first principles: unity and diversity . . . Unity is God; diversity is nothing other than Hylê . . .'. On other twelfth-century expositions, cf. 'New approaches to the School of Chartres', in my *Intellectuals and Poets in Medieval Europe* (Rome, 1992), esp. pp. 33-39.

[25] See most recently R. C. Dales, *Medieval Discussions of the Eternity of the World* (Leiden, 1990); R. C. Dales, O. Argerami (edd.), *Medieval Latin Texts on the Eternity of the World* (Leiden, 1991).

[26] Ed. N. J. Green-Pedersen, in *Boethii Daci* (cit. Ch. II n. 54), pp. 333-66. Green-Pedersen (p. xx) dates the *De aeternitate mundi* ca. 1270.

[27] I am not of course suggesting that the extant *Convivio* is a seamless garment. Not only discontinuities but anomalies remain, both between treatises and within them. It is hard, for instance, to reconcile the supreme felicity of contemplation, proclaimed in treatises III and IV, with the analogies Dante draws between the heavens and the sciences at II, xiv: there Metaphysics is likened to the Milky

look more closely at certain continuities of theme and content between treatises III and IV, which I would argue are just as compelling and just as vital to the larger design as the changes that Dante himself signals. After that, I should like to suggest something which may seem far more surprising. For all their divergences of style and manner and matter, I would see one other important feature binding the third and fourth treatises together. Their prose is poetic in a particular way in which that of the first two is not. The prose of III and IV is not only rich in imagery, but the images in both are used symphonically. In III it is a symphony of Solomonic imagery and images of love-worship, all the beauty and radiance, terror and awe, longings and joys of amorous union that she can embody and arouse, she who is daughter of God, bride of the Emperor of heaven, companion, mistress and beloved. In IV it is a symphony of images of organic fertility: the seed, shoot and bud, leaves and fronds, flowers and fruit; the planting, germination, growth, blossoming, and final ripeness. When I call these ranges of imagery symphonic, I mean not only that they have intrinsic imaginative coherence, but that the individual images set up further harmonies among one another and for one another, so that their sum in these two treatises is more than the expressions that make them up — just as a symphony is more than the sum of its notes.

Concentrating on some thoughts about these continuities of theme and imagery means that I can say little or nothing about certain other topics for which *Convivio* IV and its canzone are renowned: the false definition of nobility which Dante ascribes to Emperor Frederick II, for instance, or Dante's discussion of the basis of imperial authority, which was to loom so large in his *Monarchia*. These indeed belong with the major themes of the fourth treatise — but they are themes that have long received much expert analysis.[28] From out of the density and multifariousness of argument in *Convivio* IV, I have chosen instead certain other motifs and images which have had rather less attention, where some new light can still perhaps be shed.

The most essential continuity between *Convivio* III and IV lies in the rôle of the Donna Gentile herself. In IV she is celebrated in ways that often depart from those

Way in the heaven of the stars, but Moral Philosophy to the still higher heaven, the Crystalline, for, 'if Moral Philosophy ceased, the other sciences would be hidden for a time, and there would be neither generation of felicity nor the life of felicity' (II, xiv, 18). Any attempt to impose extra neatness, to smoothe over every incongruity in Dante's incomplete 'work in progress', would be self-defeating. This is a different matter, however, from arguing, like Corti, that there is a fundamental ideological change perceptible in the fourth treatise. In particular, I cannot see that the attitude to the Donna Gentile and to the ideals she represents in II-III is in any way undermined or compromised in IV.

[28] See the fine recent bibliography in Dante, *Monarchia*, tr. and ed. Prue Shaw (Cambridge, 1995), esp. the sections 'Dante and politics' and 'Dante and empire' (pp. 155-56). The outstanding contributions, in my view, are those of (in alphabetical order) Davis, Kantorowicz, Nardi, and Vinay. Not mentioned here, and indeed little known, is one remarkable older translation and discussion: Wolfram von den Steinen, *Heilige und Helden des Mittelalters. Dante, Die Monarchie* (Breslau, 1926).

of III, but that steadily complement them. At the close of IV, i Dante makes explicit:

By my lady, as always, I mean her who was the subject of the preceding discussion, namely that light most full of power, Filosofia, whose beams make the flowers renew their fronds and fructify the true nobility of human beings . . .[29]

The sentence enacts the transition from the imagery of loving radiance to that of fecundity.

In the next chapter, to explain how the Donna once again appeared 'disdainful and fierce' in her attitude to him, Dante refers us back to III, x, where, as we saw, he treated the seeming ferocity and scorn she showed in the ballata *Voi che savete* as a delusion caused 'by a sickness of [my] soul, which was impassioned by too much desire'. At the close of *Convivio* IV, ii Dante deepens the meaning of the image in the ballata, where the Donna seemed to account for her lack of gentleness through having passed from feeling the shafts of Love to gazing at Love's reflection in her own eyes. She will not show outgoing sympathy to others: she has made herself self-sufficient in her contemplation. So too in the canzone of *Convivio* IV the first strophe concludes:

E, cominciando, chiamo quel signore
ch'a la mia donna ne li occhi dimora,
per ch'ella di se stessa s'innamora.

And at the outset, I call upon that lord
who dwells in my lady's eyes,
so that she enamours herself of herself.

In the prose of IV, ii Dante (who had just claimed that in this treatise he would eschew allegory!) also explains that the Donna's lord is Truth, who dwells in the eyes, that is, in the demonstrations, of Filosofia; she falls in love with herself because 'she turns her gaze back on herself when the beauty of her lord's eyes appears to her'; and this means, Dante goes on, that 'the soul, philosophizing, contemplates not only this Truth but contemplates her own act of contemplating and its beauty, reflecting on herself and falling in love with herself because of the beauty of her initial contemplation'.[30]

Dante, it is plain, has said goodbye neither to allegory nor to that stream of Neoplatonic speculation which emerged in some of the highest moments of

[29] *Conv.* IV, i, 11: 'Per mia donna intendo sempre quella che ne la precedente ragione è ragionata, cioè quella luce virtuosissima, Filosofia, li cui raggi fanno li fiori rifronzire e fruttificare la verace de li uomini nobilitade . . .'. The syntax is of a complexity matching that of the image. I accept Simonelli's suggestion (*Materiali*, cit. Ch. II n. 21), that no addition is necessary before *li fiori*, whether *[ne] li fiori*, as in the older editions, or *[dal]li fiori* (thus Ageno, p. 264). Vasoli (ad loc., p. 533) valuably notes the anticipation here of the final image of *Purgatorio* (33, 143 f.).

[30] *Conv.* IV, ii, 17-18.

Convivio III. Once more I would suggest a passage in Albert the Great's *Super Ethica* as the likeliest stimulus to Dante's conceit. Commenting on Aristotle's remarkable phrase, 'It would seem that contemplation alone is loved for its own sake' (*Videbitur . . . ipsa sola propter seipsam diligi*)[31] — a phrase that Thomas, in his commentary, ignores — Albert, who defines the possession of truth as 'the felicity most sufficient in itself' (*felicitas sufficientissima per se*),[32] confronts an objection that

> enjoyment is fulfilled in love, for it consists in the beholding of what is possessed and loved; but in contemplation there is enjoyment of felicity, because it is a delight; therefore contemplation is ordered towards a love beyond itself.[33]

Albert answers in a way that helps to show how Dante's Donna Gentile can find the fulfilment of love and of truth in her own eyes. He says:

> loving and possessing what is beheld both result from beholding and are in what is beheld — thus it does not follow that beholding is ordered towards something else, beyond itself.[34]

All animals, men and beasts, according to Aristotle, have a natural component of self-love. But Dante sees a way in which human beings can imitate the more sublime intellectual self-love of the Donna Gentile. Their desire comes to love more deeply their nobler part, the mind:

> Thus, if the mind always takes delight in the use of what is loved — for this is the fruit of love — the use of our mind is supremely delightful to us. And what is supremely delightful to us is our felicity and our beatitude . . .[35]

At this point Dante, for the first time in the *Convivio*, follows Boethius of Dacia in affirming a twofold use of our mind, practical as well as speculative. Each use is most delightful (*dilettosissimo*), though the speculative one more so. The practical use is to bring things about virtuously, through our own power, with prudence, temperance, fortitude and justice. The speculative use is to contemplate the works of God and nature. In both lies our beatitude and the summit of felicity. Yet the speculative, the exercise without admixture of our noblest part, cannot have its use perfectly in this life — it will have that in God, who is the supreme

[31] *Ethica*, X, 7, 1177b, 1.

[32] *Super Ethica* (cit. Ch. II n. 64), p. 755b, 43.

[33] Ibid. p. 754a, 12-15: '. . . fruitio completur in amore; est enim visio habiti et amati; sed in contemplatione felicitatis est fruitio, quia delectatio; ergo contemplatio ipsa ordinatur ulterius ad amorem'.

[34] Ibid. p. 754a, 38-41: '. . . amare et habere visum sunt consequentia visionem et sunt in eodem, et ideo non sequitur, quod visio ordinetur ad aliquid aliud'.

[35] *Conv.* IV, xxii, 9.

intelligible — except insofar as in this life it contemplates God and gazes at him through his effects.[36]

This thought seems to me to match perfectly the qualifications with which Dante had hedged the supreme earthly contemplative felicity in the third treatise: 'no delight in this life is so great that it can take away the thirst from our soul . . . for contentment in paradise is perpetual, which this contentment can by no means be'.[37] Nonetheless, as we saw, the third treatise also includes hints of a different nuance — experiencing even on earth, in the Donna Gentile's demonstrations and persuasions, the highest joy of felicity, which is the greatest good in paradise. So too we read in the fourth treatise, with explicit reference back to the third, as well as to Averroes, that 'the desire for knowledge is natural, so that there is a certain end in which it is fulfilled'.[38] The emphasis fluctuates similarly in both treatises; hence I cannot accept Corti's claim that 'as regards the notion of felicity, Dante changes his opinion',[39] renouncing in the fourth treatise that unconditional commitment to the Donna Gentile which he had shown in the third.

To explain how the contemplative felicity surpasses the active, and is the highest manifestation of human nobility, Dante develops a philosophical allegory whose details are unparalleled,[40] out of an episode in the Gospel of Mark. There the three Maries go to the monument to find the Saviour, and find instead a young man in white. He bids them tell the disciples that the Saviour will precede them to Galilee: 'there you shall see him'. To cite from Dante's allegorical reading:

> These three women can signify the three schools of the active life, that is, the Epicureans, Stoics, and Peripatetics. They go to the monument, that is, to the present world, the receptacle of corruptible things,[41] and ask for the Saviour, that is, felicity, and do not find it; but they find a young man who is robed in white . . .

[36] Ibid. 10-13.

[37] See above, p. 42.

[38] *Conv.* IV, xiii, 7-8 (I give the phrase in its context): 'our natural desires, as is shown above in the third treatise, move towards a certain end; and the desire for knowledge is natural, so that there is a certain end in which it is fulfilled, even if few reach the end of the day's journey, because the rest take a bad road. And whoever understands the Commentator (i.e. Averroes) on *De anima* Book III understands this through him'.

[39] See above, p. 52.

[40] As Vasoli (p. 791) rightly observes, the lengthy allegory of the same text by Hugh of St Cher, which was cited in the Busnelli-Vandelli edition, II, 284 f., does little to illuminate Dante's reading. According to Hugh, the monument is Scripture, the three women are students of Scripture who, finding it hard, ask, who will roll away the difficulties? They see a young man, who is a doctor or prelate of the Church, and who tells them that the Lord will be seen only in Galilee — that is, in the heavenly home, after death, or else, after their transmigration from vices to virtues.

While it is quite likely that Dante was familiar with some edifying constructs of this kind, that of Hugh is hardly at Dante's level of inspiration.

[41] Compare the allegory in Bernardus Silvestris' commentary on the *Aeneid* (cit. Ch. II n. 75), p. 27: when the image of Anchises, allegorically the divine Father, urges Aeneas to descend to the underworld (*ad inferos descendere*): 'in this Aeneas is urged to descend to the things of this world (*mundana*), by way of cognition; there he will see the Father, for, though the Father dwells on high, a cognition of the

This angel is this nobility of ours which comes from God . . . which speaks within our reason, and says to each of these sects, that is, to whoever goes seeking felicity in the active life, that it is not here; but let them go, and tell the disciples . . . that felicity will precede us in Galilee, that is, in speculation.

Galilee (the name was traditionally derived from Greek γάλα, 'milk') is the white radiance of contemplation. The felicity 'will precede' the seekers there, because its supreme form can never be reached fully here.[42]

Dante's reading of the Gospel episode is an allegory in the rhetorical sense familiar from Quintilian:[43] it is a single metaphor, continued and extended to each aspect of the brief narrative. What makes it captivating is, first of all, its sheer unexpectedness. As Aristotle argues in the *Poetics*: 'making good metaphors depends on perceiving the similarity in dissimilars'. This, he declares, 'is the only thing that cannot be learnt from others; it is a sign of native genius'.[44]

There is only one author in the western Middle Ages, to my knowledge, who attempted comparably unpredictable philosophical allegories of certain Gospel episodes: Hildegard of Bingen, whose set of 'Gospel interpretations', written in the 1150s, shows the same sweeping freedom of perception and invention.[45] Her text, however, survives only in two manuscripts, of Rhenish provenance, and will have been little known.

But in Dante's allegory the thrill of recognition of the similar in dissimilars — the quest of the three philosophical schools in that of the three Maries — is deepened, I would suggest, by a further recognition. This passage in the fourth

Creator can nonetheless be obtained by way of comparison, by consideration of the frailty (*fragilitate*) of temporal things'.

[42] *Conv.* IV, xxii, 14-18.

[43] *Institutio oratoria*, VIII, 6, 44-50.

[44] *Poetics*, 1459a, 4-8.

[45] I have tried to show this with some detailed illustrations in an essay, 'Platonic-Christian Allegories in the Homilies of Hildegard of Bingen', in *From Athens to Chartres: Neoplatonism and Medieval Thought. Studies in Honour of Édouard Jeauneau*, ed. H. J. Westra (Leiden, 1992), pp. 381-96. The essay's epigraph is the passage from Aristotle's *Poetics* just cited.

Though Hildegard's two homilies on the episode in Mark belong with her theological and moral, rather than her philosophical, ones, the second is nonetheless of interest in relation to Dante, in that Hildegard too has a moment of imaginative profundity which arises as if unpremeditatedly. (I am not of course suggesting a direct link between her text and his.) For Hildegard, the three Maries are three faculties within the human being: the knowledge of good and evil, rationality, and physical delight (*scientia boni et mali*, *rationalitas*, *gustus carnis*). The young man who greets them, in the monument of good desire (*bonum desiderium*), is another life (*alia vita*). He tells them that God is not here, 'because now he is not buried in you, as he was before'; yet he will precede them, 'preparing you an eternal dwelling'. What is striking is the perception of the divine first as embedded, or buried (*sepultus*), in the three human powers, and then as leading the human being beyond desire to a superhuman goal. These two moments may allude to Fall and Redemption, yet the basic meaning of Hildegard's reading seems to be an interior one, not confined by the established theological pattern.

The text as printed by J. B. Pitra, *Analecta Sacra*, VIII (Montecassino, 1882), 283 f., should be corrected esp. at the following places from the principal MS, Hessische Landesbibl. 2, fols. 449vb-450rb: l. 8, for *Iudaei* read *fidei*; 9, for *solo* read *sole*; 11, for *invicem* read *ad invicem*.

treatise echoes, complements and completes the equally unexpected, equally daring projection in the third, where the Donna Gentile inspires the faith, hope and charity that will lead to a philosophical concord, to that celestial Athens which unites Stoics, Peripatetics and Epicureans, through the light of eternal truth.[46]

As the earlier passage is brought to mind, we understand that this light of eternal truth was what is now named Galilee, and that what Dante had envisioned there was the completion of the quest, the full attainment of the felicity. In the later allegory we see the three groups of pagan philosophers, like the three Maries, while they are still active and their seeking is still incomplete, still facing setbacks. Yet Galilee, like the celestial Athens, gives grounds for optimism to all, however beclouded their longing for felicity may have been: if guided by nobility, the angel within, the search will lead to the harmony of contemplation. The celestial Athens, the utopian harmony of the three pagan schools, is achieved by the three theological virtues — faith, hope and charity — which the Donna Gentile inspires; and we can perceive these same pagan schools in the allegory of the three Maries, at the theological moment of redemption that follows upon Christ's resurrection. Pagan and Christian concepts and images are reflected in each other, even as the truth is reflected and loved by the Donna Gentile in her own eyes.

In the earlier part of his exposition in *Convivio* IV, Dante uses many-branched arguments to demolish what he sees as the false conceptions of nobility — all those that would link it not with the angel within but with riches or ancestry. Even Emperor Frederick II — to whom Dante ascribes the view that nobility means possession of ancient wealth together with beautiful manners — is not spared: Dante demonstrates at length that here Frederick was not pronouncing in a sphere where he had any valid jurisdiction. And even if Frederick's view is also the majority view, and if Aristotle, 'the master of human reason', says that what seems so to the majority cannot be entirely false, here again Dante stoutly defends his own position, with a *distinguo*: Aristotle, when he said that, was referring to rational opinion, not opinion based merely on sensory evidence.[47] Such opinion can always delude, and it is to this that the popular (and imperial) view of nobility belongs.

Soon after coping with Aristotle, Dante has a passage distinguishing the senses in which the desire for riches and the desire for knowledge can each be called insatiable, a passage that Nardi justly singled out as 'one of the most beautiful pages of philosophical literature of all time'.[48] Here too Dante's analysis both demolishes and goes beyond the clichés of popular opinion. His illustrations are lighthearted ('we see little ones longing most of all for an apple; then, somewhat

[46] See above, pp. 24, 35.
[47] *Conv.* IV, viii, 6.
[48] *Dal 'Convivio' alla 'Commedia'* (cit. n. 12), p. 76.

later, longing for a little bird; then, later still, for a fine suit; then for a horse, and then for a woman'),[49] but by way of these he arrives at a series of distinctions which, though stimulated by Boethius, lead him to his own impassioned account of the unique structure of the desire for knowledge. When at last, in IV, xx, Dante reaches his own definition of nobility — the source of that never-ceasing contemplative desire — the imagery of fecundity of which I spoke comes to predominate.[50]

Neither this imagery nor Dante's definition itself is Aristotelian:

> . . . *to some*, that is to those who have understanding, who are few, it is manifest that human nobility is nothing otner than 'the seed of felicity' *placed by God in the well disposed soul*, that is, the soul whose body is perfectly adjusted to it in every way. For if the virtues are the fruit of nobility, and felicity is the sweetness attained through these, it is manifest that this nobility is the seed of felicity . . .[51]

What may have stimulated Dante's image of the divinely placed seed, as Vasoli rightly noted, is once more a passage in Boethius' *Consolation of Philosophy*, one that had already given a cue to some of the troubadours in their lyrical debates about the nature of nobility, as well as to Alan of Lille.[52] It is a brief poem in which Boethius says:

> The whole human race on earth stems from a like origin,
> for all things have a single Father, one alone governs all.
> He gave the sun his rays and gave the moon her crescent,
> he allotted men to earth as he did stars to heaven;
> he enclosed minds, brought down from his high throne, in bodies.
> Therefore a noble shoot brings forth all mortals.
> Why brag about your race and ancestry? If you look at your beginnings,
> and at your author, God, no one is base —
> unless, fostering the worse through vice, he abandons his own origin.[53]

[49] *Conv.* IV, xii, 16.

[50] This imagery develops from IV, xvi, where the defining of nobility is first broached

[51] *Conv.* IV, xx, 9 (the words italicized are cited from the canzone): '. . . *ad alquanti*, cioè a quelli che hanno intelletto, che sono pochi, è manifesto che nobilitade umana non sia altro che "seme di felicitade", *messo da Dio ne l'anima ben posta*, cioè lo cui corpo è d'ogni parte disposto perfettamente. Ché se le vertudi sono frutto di nobilitade, e felicitade è dolcezza [per quelle] comparata, manifesto è essa nobilitade essere semente di felicitade . . .'.

[52] Cf. Alain de Lille, *Anticlaudianus* (ed. Robert Bossuat, Paris, 1955), esp. VIII 397-IX 146. On the *Anticlaudianus* in relation to Dante, see my *Dante and Medieval Latin Traditions* (cit. n. 19), Ch. I (ii): 'Alan of Lille: Poetry and Creativity', and the entries under *Anticlaudianus* in the index to Vasoli, p. 1056. One passage I should like to add. When Dante writes (*Conv.* IV, xxi, 10):

> And some are of the opinion that if all the mentioned virtues accorded in their best disposition in the production of a soul, so much of godhead would descend into that soul that it would almost be another God incarnate. And this is almost all that can be said in natural terms.

this seems to me virtually a précis of the central argument of Alan's epic: the production of the *novus homo*. (Only God's direct intervention, in the giving of the soul, is not mentioned here.)

[53] *Cons. Phil.* III m. 6:

Boethius has the image of the *nobile germen* (the noble shoot, or bud), and for him this is a nobility that depends purely on the divine origin of the human mind. Thus it belongs to the whole human race. This, its intrinsic nobility, is given; the essential human nobility consists in living aware of one's celestial origin, that is, in living virtuously. Only the vicious are ignoble.

Thus for Boethius, as for Dante, nobility in this sense is a quality of being, found in individuals, and not a matter of lineage. Yet his thoughts, which may well have acted as a catalyst for Dante's, are not wholly like these either. Boethius does not link his *nobile germen* with the Aristotelian felicity of contemplation, nor yet, like Dante, with a celestial grace, a 'blessed and divine infusion'.[54] Boethius, unlike Dante, does not extend his notion of a nobility of heavenly origin to other species,[55] nor again does he claim that the worldlier, widely accepted notion of nobility is pernicious and should be eradicated. In the prose immediately preceding these Boethian verses, Philosophia argues not that the commonly received notion is false, merely that it is trivial and of only limited usefulness:

> Who does not see how vain, how futile is the title of nobility? . . . It seems to be a certain praise deriving from our parents' merits . . . If there is any good in nobility, I think it is only this, that a necessity would seem to be imposed upon the noble, lest their nobility degenerate from the virtue of their ancestors.[56]

Boethius does not develop the image of the *nobile germen* elsewhere in the *Consolation*. Dante's images of fertility, by contrast, with all their variants and interactions, are used in the entire second half of *Convivio* IV, and come increasingly to colour his choice of language.

When in IV, xvi Dante argues that nobility means the perfection, in every kind of being, of its own nature, he adds that the finest perfection in any species must be defined and known through its effects. 'By their fruits you shall know them'. With this phrase from Matthew we approach Dante's web of language of planting and growing, flowering and bearing fruit. The human fruits, this chapter

> Omne hominum genus in terris simili surgit ab ortu.
> Unus enim rerum pater est, unus cuncta ministrat.
> Ille dedit Phoebo radios, dedit et cornua lunae,
> ille homines etiam terris dedit ut sidera caelo;
> hic clausit membris animos celsa sede petitos:
> mortales igitur cunctos edit nobile germen.
> Quid genus et proavos strepitis? Si primordia vestra
> auctoremque deum spectes, nullus degener exstat
> ni vitiis peiora fovens propriam deserat ortum.

[54] *Conv.* IV, xx, 7.

[55] Unless this should be implied in the phrase *Haec igitur Sapientia cuncto equidem animarum generi meritum suae divinitatis inponit* ('In every kind of soul this Wisdom therefore imprints the reward of her divinity'), in his first commentary on Porphyry, cited above, p. 29.

[56] *Cons. Phil.* III pr. 6, 20-29.

concludes, 'are the moral and intellectual virtues, of which our nobility is the seed'.

The moral virtues, which bring felicity in the active life, are fruits that (in the words of the canzone) stem from a single root. These virtues and their nature are now expounded in terms of Aristotle's *Ethics* — yet Dante's attempt to show inductively that all of them proceed from nobility, as effects do from their cause, is not Aristotelian but of his own devising. As 'the tree trunk (*lo piè de l'albero*), which contains all the other branches, must be called their principle and cause . . . so too with nobility, which contains every virtue'.[57]

In Chapter xix, nobility becomes 'a heaven in which many and diverse stars' of virtues shine, so that 'certainly it is no cause for marvel if they bring about many and diverse fruits in human nobility: so many are its natures and its powers, on which, as on diverse branches, the fruit grows'. Our first 'cause for marvel' here might be Dante's boldness in mixing the metaphors of stars and fruits. Underlying the conflation is a certain belief in celestial influences: these can effect fruitful growth in the human as in the natural sphere. And (even though Dante does not dwell on it expressly here) we should recall that one group of these influences, in the Neoplatonic-Christian cosmos, is the order of angels named 'Virtues' (the *Virtuti* of *Convivio* II, v, 6). That Dante's imagination has in fact leapt from stars to angels becomes clear in his continuation, in a thought as buoyant as it is unprecedented: 'In truth I dare to say that human nobility, in that it has *many* fruits, surpasses that of the angel (even if the angelic nature is more divine in its unity)'.[58]

Each chapter that follows widens the associations of the language of fertile growth. Nobility is a matter of grace, not race (IV, xx): while the canzone tells, it is a divine gift, which can make those who are given it godlike, in the prose Dante adds that 'the divine seed does not descend into a family-tree or stock (*stirpe*) . . . the stock does not make the individuals noble — it is they who ennoble the stock'. There is an ironic contrast implicit between the *stirpe* of a famous family and the trunk of the fruitful tree of the virtues.

Dante then treats the descent of the seed of nobility into the human soul from both a philosophical and a theological perspective. The first — his account of the origin and formation of the soul, a discussion renewed and given its final unfolding in *Purgatorio* 25 — is one of the summits of Dante's philosophical speculation, and one where Nardi has brilliantly shown the poet's deeply informed, eclectic individuality.[59] The second perspective — the infusion of grace into the soul in the gifts of the Holy Ghost — is presented more briefly, but it culminates once more in the images of organic growth and fecundity, which are here invoked rapturously:

[57] *Conv.* IV, xviii, 5.
[58] *Conv.* IV, xix, 6.
[59] See especially the essay 'L'origine dell'anima umana secondo Dante', in his *Studi di filosofia medievale* (Rome, 1960), pp. 9-68.

Oh how good the crops, and good and lovable the seed! and oh how admirable and benign the sower, who waits only for human nature to prepare the soil for the sowing! And blessed those who cultivate such a seed fittingly![60]

After the jubilant cries, the meticulous allegorical unfolding. The first and noblest shoot that sprouts from this seed, as it strives to become fruitful, is the mind's appetite. This shoot can be cultivated and made to grow firm by good habit, it can strengthen itself in upright growth so that it may be able to bear fruit, and that from its fruit the sweetness of human felicity may spring.[61]

The figurative presentation is taken further in the next chapter (IV, xxii), just before the allegory of the three Maries at the monument. In the practical and the speculative use of our mind lies our beatitude and highest felicity — and this is the sweetness of the seed. Many times, however, such a seed does not attain that sweetness, if it has been poorly cultivated or the shoots have grown wild. Yet even where the seed does not fall at the outset, one may still induce germination, so that at last there is fruit. With moving optimism Dante adds, there is a way (even if it's seldom taken) of engrafting a new nature, as it were, upon a root of a different kind; and that our noblest part, the intellect, is lovable most of all 'because of its radical love' (*per lo radicale amore*).[62]

Such imagery still recurs several times in the course of Dante's evocation, subtle and affectionate — though also, one must admit, thoroughly male-oriented — of the qualities through which nobility shows itself in the four ages of human life. At the very beginning of our existence, the divine seed, nobility, burgeons (*germoglia*) in each of the soul's powers, vegetative, sensitive and rational; then it branches (*dibrancasi*) through these, perfecting their capacities, till the immortal part of the soul returns heavenward, to the highest and most glorious sower.[63]

In the first stage of life (*adolescenza*), Nature gives us what we need in order to enter life well, 'as we see that she gives the vine leaves for the protection of the fruit, and tendrils . . . so that it can bear the weight of its fruit'.[64] Or again, the perfection that is acquired in the second stage of life (*gioventute*) should extend its radiance to others in the third: 'the human being should then open, almost like

[60] *Conv.* IV, xxi, 12. For the first exclamation — *Oh buone biade, e buona e amabile sementa!* — I follow Ageno's earlier suggestion (cited by Vasoli *ad loc.*) of reading *amabile* and not *ammirabile*. As she noted, some MSS do have *amabile* here, and *ammirabile* could be an early scribe's anticipation of this word in the exclamation that follows (*e oh ammirabile e benigno seminatore . . .*). In her text, however, Ageno (p. 394) prints *amirabile* (*sic*) in both exclamations.

[61] *Conv.* IV, xxi, 13-14.

[62] *Conv.* IV, xxii, 13. I take this phrase to mean, 'because of its love for the root from which all the virtues spring', and the words *che detto è* (ibid.) to refer back to the canzone, vv. 81-82:

> Dico ch'ogni vertù principalmente
> vien da una radice.

[63] *Conv.* IV, xxiii, 3.

[64] *Conv.* IV, xxiv, 10.

a rose that can no longer remain closed, and should diffuse the scent which has been generated within'. The prudence of this later age (*senettute*) gives counsel even without request, 'as the rose gives its scent not only to one who goes to it for that, but even to whoever draws near it'.[65] In the fourth age (*senio*), the dominant image is that of the good sailor navigating back to his harbour, God; yet to evoke the gentleness of dying well, 'for in such a death as this there is no pain nor any harshness', Dante reverts to another image from organic life: 'just as a ripe apple detaches itself lightly and without violence from its branch, so our soul parts without suffering from the body where it has been'.[66]

I am only too aware that, in trying to indicate some of the modulations of the language of growth and fruitfulness in these resonant chapters, other languages, other harmonies, other ideas have had to be passed in silence. Yet I would suggest that there is a motivically ordered quality in this language and imagery which makes it insidiously symphonic in the sense I described. The melodies are perhaps easier to recognize at first in the spectacular Solomonic imagery, the language of love-worship, which pervades the third treatise, yet gradually they become audible and traceable in the fourth as well. These melodies in the language and imagery of the two treatises help to show how Dante's loving quest for the Donna Gentile and his loving quest for Nobility have deliberately been made in some measure parallel.

What then is the import, ultimately, of the symphonic languages of love and fruitfulness? Both are transfused by a longing for that condition which Boethius in his prison had longed for, and had called *felicitas* and *beatitudo* — Dante's *felicitade* and *beatitudine* — for which the usual modern English rendering, 'happiness', seems too shallow and inadequate. Neither Boethius, condemned to death, nor Dante, condemned to exile, knew 'happiness' in the commonly accepted sense. Yet *de profundis* each embarked upon a quest, poignant and heroic, for inner felicity. The love-language celebrating the Donna Gentile conveys Dante's quest for intellectual peace within himself; his language of seed and fruit, celebrating Nobility, conveys his quest for an organic beatitude. At the same time it leaps to view that neither Boethius nor Dante was a quietist: by the record of their quest they longed to change the outlook and the values of their fellow-men.

To conclude, I should like to turn briefly to the close of the final chapter of the fourth treatise — the close, that is, of the *Convivio* as it survives. Dante at last comes to speak of the envoi — the *tornata* — of his song, his own, poetic, *Contra-Gentiles*. It is now perfect, and hence must go to reveal its mission wherever the Donna Gentile, Philosophy, shall be found:

[65] *Conv.* IV, xxvii, 4 and 7.

[66] *Conv.* IV, xxviii, 4.

This most noble lady will be found when her chamber is found, that is, the soul in which she lodges. And Philosophy lodges not only in the wise, but also, as is proved above in another treatise, she is wherever the love of her is lodged . . .

And I say to the canzone: 'Tell this lady, I go about speaking of your friend'. Nobility is indeed her friend — for they love each other so much that Nobility is always seeking her company, and Philosophy does not turn her sweetest gaze anywhere else. Oh how great and how beautiful an adornment is this, which is given to Nobility in the last part of this song, calling her the friend of her whose own principle of being lies in the most secret part of the divine mind![67]

This final, triumphant outcry, which crowns the work as it survives, comes after many that are equally passionate but very different in tone. In the first treatise, Dante's threnody of exile and poverty had begun with a pang of regret: 'Ah if only it had pleased the ruler of the universe that the cause of my excuse had never existed!' — the excuse here being that the disgrace of exile has led him to write a work profound and demanding enough to rehabilitate him in men's eyes.[68] In the third treatise come two pairs of exclamations — each a jubilant

[67] *Conv.* IV, xxx, 5-6:

Allora si troverà questa donna nobilissima quando si truova la sua camera, cioè l'anima in cui essa alberga. Ed essa Filosofia non solamente alberga pur ne li sapienti, ma eziandio, come provato è di sopra in altro trattato, essa è dovunque alberga l'amore di quella . . .

E dico ad essa: Dì a questa donna, *'Io vo parlando de l'amica vostra'*. Bene è sua amica Nobilitate; ché tanto l'una con l'altra s'ama, che Nobilitate sempre la dimanda, e Filosofia non volge lo sguardo suo dolcissimo a l'altra parte. Oh quanto e come bello adornamento è questo che ne l'ultimo di questa canzone si dà ad essa, chiamandola amica di quella la cui propria ragione è nel secretissimo de la divina mente!

I have followed Ageno (p. 456) in capitalizing Filosofia and Nobilitate, but have not adopted her emendations or her postulated lacuna in this passage.

Here Dante, at the close of the treatise, returns fully to the metaphorics of Sapientia. The allegory of Filosofia and Nobilitate and their lodging was foreshadowed conceptually at *Conv.* III, ii, 14-16; the human soul, 'by the *nobility* of its ultimate power, that is, reason, shares in the divine nature in the guise of sempiternal intelligence, because the soul is so much *ennobled* in that sovereign power, and so much denuded of matter, that the divine light radiates in it as if in an angel; because of this, philosophers call the human being a divine animal. In this *noblest* part of the soul are several faculties (*vertudi*) . . . Thus it is manifest that by 'mind' one understands this ultimate and *noblest* part of the soul'.

Both this passage and the concluding one, it seems to me, may well owe something to yet another moment in Albert the Great's commentary *Super Ethica*, Bk. X (cit. Ch. II n. 64). To deal with the objection 'that contemplative felicity is not in accordance with the power of the [human] intellect (*secundum potentiam intellectus*)', Albert answers:

The noblest aspect (*Nobilissimum*) of a lower nature is where it has its contact with a higher one . . . but human nature attains the nature of the Intelligences in intellectuality (*intellectualitate*); therefore that is the noblest thing (*nobilissimum*) in the human being, and thus contemplative felicity must be in accordance with the [human] intellect. (pp. 748b, 64-65, 91-95; 749a, 1-3)

This answer clearly reveals its debt to ps-Dionysius, *De div. nom.* 4, where, in his Latin translation (P. L. 122, 1133D), Eriugena introduced the term *intellectualitas* for the highest aspect of human cognition. (It had been used only once before, but with a more general sense of 'understanding', by Tertullian, *De anima*, 38, 6). The later Dionysian translators, Johannes Sarracenus and Robert Grosseteste, retained Eriugena's term.

[68] *Conv.* I, iii, 3.

shout completed by its dark converse. The long demonstration of how the sun revolves concludes with Dante's paean, 'Oh ineffable Wisdom that ordained it thus . . .!', leading to the quasi-prophetic denunciation of his readership: 'And you, for whose benefit and delight I write, in what blindness you live, not lifting your eyes up to these things . . .!'.[69] Similarly, the joyous blessing of the Donna Gentile's devotees — 'Oh noblest and most excellent heart that is intent upon the bride of the Emperor of heaven . . .!' — is followed, not long afterwards, by the scornful challenge that begins, 'Oh worse than dead, you who shun her friendship . . .'.[70]

But it is in the fourth treatise that the heated interjections become numerous. Once more there is a conjunction of blessing (of divine providence) and anathema (against those who question it): 'Oh ineffable and incomprehensible wisdom of God . . .! And oh most foolish and most vile beasts, you that pasture in human guise . . . A curse on you and your presumption, and on whoever believes you!'.[71] For the most part, however, sheer bitter exclamations now pass like tremors of anguish through the text, above all in the final chapters. 'Oh you wretches who rule today, and oh most wretched you who are ruled! . . . Look around you, you enemies of God, you who have seized the rods of government in Italy! . . . riderless . . . wretched Italy, left without any means of government!'.[72] Most startling, perhaps, is that in Chapters xxvii and xxviii the serene, beautiful reflections on the qualities of old age are pierced by such stabs of pain and rage. It is right, Dante tells, that old age (*senetta*) should be just; the ancient philosophers saw justice appearing perfectly at that time of life, and hence the ruling of cities was entrusted to the 'Senate', the college of the old. And then: 'Oh wretched, wretched native city of mine! How great a pity rends me because of you, each time I read, each time I write, anything that relates to civil government!'.[73] There is a note here that is not far from Christ's compassionate yet ominous laments, 'Jerusalem, Jerusalem . . .'.[74]

Again, in the composed depiction of preparing for death in the last age of life (the navigator lowering his sails, the ripe apple gently dropping), there is a sudden vehemence against the old who are still full of worldly ambitions: 'Oh you wretched and vile ones, you who race to this harbour in full sail, and, where you should be resting, become shipwrecked in the blast . . .!'.[75] And even the allegory of the widowed Marcia, who chooses to die as the spouse not of a human husband (figured by Hortensius) but of the divine one (figured by Cato), culminates in the savage cry: 'Oh you ill-starred, ill-begotten ones, who would

[69] *Conv.* III, v, 22.
[70] *Conv.* III, xii, 22; III, xv, 17.
[71] *Conv.* IV, v, 9.
[72] *Conv.* IV, vi, 19-20; IV, ix, 10.
[73] *Conv.* IV, xxvii, 11.
[74] Matthew 23, 30; Luke 13, 34.
[75] *Conv.* IV, xxviii, 7.

rather depart from this life under the name of Hortensius than of Cato!'.[76] Not only Christ's laments but Christ's maledictions in the Gospels spring to mind.

Nothing, however, darkens the final chapter of the *Convivio*, which brings Nobility and Philosophy together, and closes exultantly. In that close, I would suggest, the unity of intention of the third and fourth treatises also emerges decisively. As I indicated by my only half playful choice of title for this chapter, it is a unity of ethics and aesthetics.

It is significant that only in the final chapter of the prose does Nobility become fully personified. At the last, we could say, Dante sets her ontologically on a par with the Donna Gentile. There is something not wholly serious about that parity, yet it points towards something deeply serious too. The aesthetic adventure which had begun in the songs and sonnets of the *Vita Nuova* and had found its culmination in *Amor che nella mente mi ragiona*, the loving praises of the daughter of the Emperor of the universe, finds its conclusion in the pressing — at times ferocious at times heartrending — ethical reflections on Nobility. Nobility and the Donna Gentile — the root of Dante's ethic and the womanly incarnation of his aesthetic — are indeed inseparable. Together they circumscribe all his writing of intellection and love at this point in his life.

When Wittgenstein wrote, gnomically, 'Ethics and aesthetics are one',[77] there was an ironic, even negative, note in his phrase. Ethics and aesthetics, he was suggesting, fall outside that world which we can define and of which we can speak. Ethics and aesthetics belong to a different realm, one which, according to inclination, may be called the realm of the transcendent, the unsayable, the unverifiable, or even the meaningless.

Dante perceived the oneness of ethics and aesthetics in a rather different way. Even if the Donna Gentile's paradisal joys can in some measure be known on earth, Dante also sees them as transcendent, and — unlike Wittgenstein — he does not regard the transcendent as wholly inexpressible. If the Donna Gentile belongs essentially to the transcendent realm, Dante is equally sure that she can lodge here and now in human souls. And there, in human souls, she finds and loves and never looks away from her *amica*, her beloved friend, Nobility. And

[76] *Conv.* IV, xxviii, 19. A precedent for Dante's allegorization of the Lucan episode (*Pharsalia*, II, 326-45) has not been found (cf. Vasoli pp. 870 f.). Looking among the published glosses on this passage from the ninth century to the thirteenth, I have not come across any detail that might have spurred Dante's invention.

[77] Ludwig Wittgenstein, *Tractatus Logico-Philosophicus* (London, 1922), pp. 182 f. (*Ethik und Aesthetik sind Eins*). After the statement 'Propositions cannot express anything higher' (*Sätze können nichts Höheres ausdrücken*) in 6.42 come those of 6.421:

> It is clear that ethics cannot be expressed.
> Ethics are transcendental.
> (Ethics and aesthetics are one.)

In the newer translation by D. F. Pears and B. F. McGuinness (London-New York, 2nd corr. impr., 1963), the parenthetic sentence has been rendered 'Ethics and aesthetics are one and the same'. But this forces the meaning of *sind Eins* towards a heavy over-emphasis. The earlier version is preferable here.

this *amica* belongs essentially to our familiar world: Nobility, 'when she walks, treads on the ground'.

Excursus

THE 'REJECTION' OF THE DONNA GENTILE

A certain late Romantic mode of interpreting poetry, which I shall call 'biographism', was cultivated particularly in the later nineteenth and early twentieth century. Thus for instance, among Dante's later *Rime*, outside the *Vita Nuova* and the *Convivio*, there is a sonnet which begins:

> Due donne in cima de la mente mia
> venute sono a ragionar d'amore . . .[1]

'Two ladies have come into the summit of my mind to discourse of love.' In the ninth verse of this sonnet Dante names these ladies: they are Beauty and Virtue — *Bellezza e Virtù*. But that was not enough for the scholars addicted to biographism. In the notes to the Barbi-Pernicone edition of the *Rime* we are given a conspectus of their views.[2] Fraticelli identified the two ladies in the sonnet as Filosofia and Beatrice respectively; Witte, by contrast, as Beatrice and the Donna Gentile; Serafini, as Moral Philosophy and the shadowy Gentucca, who is alluded to only in *Purgatorio* 24, 37; Santi, as Beatrice and Gemma Donati. With the group of Dante's '*pargoletta*' songs (Foster-Boyde nos. 64-66, Barbi-Pernicone nos. 87-89), the theses multiply.[3] From the early 'Anonimo fiorentino', for whom the *pargoletta* is an unnamed 'young girl from Lucca' known to the poet Bonagiunta (*Purg*. 24, 43 ff.), to the many scholars, starting with Fraticelli, who see her as Beatrice, to Dionisi, for whom she is Sapientia, to Serafini, who yet again proposes Gentucca. For Zingarelli the *pargoletta* is a blend of the Donna Gentile and the harsh Lady Stone (Donna Pietra) of another group of Dante's lyrics, and several scholars from D'Ancona onwards believe the *pargoletta* and Donna Pietra to be one and the same — real, not allegorical — young woman.

Each of the scholars who volunteered such identifications had, I would suggest, been lured into 'the traps of believing' — *las trampas de la fe*, to adapt Octavio Paz's memorable expression.[4] These are traps which Dante, the master-strategist, has knowingly set amid his *Rime* for all those who will not consider them as self-subsistent poetic artefacts but are eager to grasp 'more'. The problem is, the biographizing 'more' quickly comes to be too much. The catalogue of the diverse attempts at biographizing comes to sound almost comical. The ventures come to seem just so much arbitrary speculation, so much fantasizing history.

[1] Foster-Boyde no. 71, Barbi-Pernicone no. 86. Both editions are cited in full above, Ch. I n. 1.
[2] Barbi-Pernicone pp. 471 f.
[3] Ibid. pp. 476 f.
[4] From the title of his study: *Sor Juana Inés de la Cruz, o Las Trampas de la Fe* (Barcelona, 1982).

Is this not too simplistic a way of trying to enter that poetic world which Dante and his poet-friends, and the young women in their circle, inhabited with imaginative adroitness? Even Beatrice's famous expression of scorn for the *pargoletta* (*Purg*. 31, 59), and her other reproaches of Dante near the close of *Purgatorio*, must be seen in the first place as part of a constructed poetic web, Beatrice's vehemence and Dante's anguish and remorse themselves as poetic-dramatic creations. They are on the same imaginative plane as the earlier emotional-intellectual creations in *Vita Nuova*, *Rime* and *Convivio*, even if still more poignant or more profound. To treat the encounter with Beatrice in *Purgatorio* as if it existed outside Dante's total poetic web, as if it could be read as the biographer's verdict on Dante's personal spiritual development — and there have been many attempts to read it thus — is once more to fall into *las trampas de la fe*.

In recent decades, the principal victim of biographism has been the Donna Gentile. In 1961 Colin Hardie identified her with the 'stammering, cross-eyed woman' who appears to Dante in a dream in *Purgatorio* (19, 7-8), and who in that dream changes into 'the sweet siren who bewitches sailors in mid-ocean', and at last has her dress torn open by Vergil, to reveal her stinking belly (19, 19-33). To support this remarkable identification, Hardie simply alluded to some passages of Dante's about the pursuit of knowledge in the prose of the *Convivio*, saying: 'The transformation by Dante's amorous gaze of the *femmina balba* into the fascinating siren corresponds to Dante's description . . . of his progress in philosophical studies, from bafflement to entire satisfaction'.[5] On the same page Hardie identified the Donna Gentile further with the prostitute (*puttana*) who is whipped by a giant in the vision in *Purgatorio* 32, 149-60. Here there is not even an attempt at finding textual support, only the assertion that 'Dante's devotion to the Donna Gentile, siren, *puttana*, had both an intellectual and an erotic element'.

In 1975 Robert Hollander went still further along this path. His point of departure was Dante's encounter with his musician-friend Casella in *Purgatorio* 2 — Casella who is able to 'console' (*consolare*, 109) Dante and Vergil and the souls newly arrived in Purgatory by singing Dante's song in praise of the Donna Gentile, *Amor che ne la mente mi ragiona*.[6] That Cato then rebuked these souls

[5] 'Beatrice's chariot in Dante's earthly paradise', *Deutsches Dante Jahrbuch*, 39 (1961), 137-72, at p. 160.

[6] See above, Ch. II n. 2, and the passage by Lino Pertile cited there. It is possible to argue with delicacy and perceptiveness that *Amor che ne la mente* is cited in *Purgatorio* 2 as a song to be transcended. This is what John Freccero does in his essay 'Casella's Song' (1973, repr. in his *Dante and the Poetics of Conversion*, Cambridge, Mass., 1986, pp. 186-94, at pp. 192, 194):

> the sudden flight of doves which were temporarily 'queti' cannot fail to signify the momentary peace to be found in this life through philosophical study ('quetar tutte mie voglie', v. 108) and the subsequent realization of a further, transcendent goal. In his scolding, Cato defines that goal in terms of *vision* . . . The 'nuova legge' (v. 106) to which Casella's song is subject is the new law, the supernatural order to which nature must ultimately give way . . . Casella's song was a respite, as was the *Convivio*; both had to be interrupted for the long journey that lay ahead.

for loitering, and commanded them to 'run to the mountain' to begin their purgation (120-24), is for Hollander the proof that 'Casella's song is a Siren's song'.[7] It is 'poisonous' and 'perverse'.[8] Hollander presents 'Dante's Lady Philosophy . . . as false Lady, as Siren . . . a wrong lady'.[9]

More recently there has been a more sophisticated interpretation of Dante's use of *Amor che ne la mente* in this canto, in Teodolinda Barolini's book *Dante's Poets*. Yet she too becomes ensnared in biographism:

> The *Convivio*'s misdirected enthusiasm for Lady Philosophy is thus replayed on the beach of Purgatory . . . Lady Philosophy was indeed a mistake.[10]

In a later essay, where Hollander claims to see 'an urgent polemic in the *Commedia* against some of the values sponsored by the *Convivio*', he refers to this as a 'predominantly American interpretive position'[11] — so perhaps I may take a well-known American citation, from *Porgy and Bess*, as epigraph for my answer:

> It ain't necessarily so.

That the character Cato reproves the souls who linger to hear Casella singing does not necessarily mean that the poet Dante rejects the content of his song *Amor che ne la mente*. Even less does it imply that Dante thereby rejects the Donna Gentile, or repudiates his *Convivio* or his ardent pursuit of Philosophy there. To read the episode in *Purgatorio* 2 in this way is not to respond to Dante's dramatic dialectic but to caricature it. It is to impose the scholar's predetermined beliefs about what Dante *ought* to be saying, about how Dante's spiritual development *ought* to have gone. In all that Dante leaves enigmatic and unsaid, the biographists profess to know 'more', with a sureness that leaves one gasping. And the 'more' they offer us is something so much more banal than what Dante offers.

As for the attempts to identify the Donna Gentile with the Siren or the prostitute in the later cantos of *Purgatorio*, not only must one repeat, 'It ain't necessarily so'. Here one must add: it needs a wilful forcing of texts in order to make it so.

If I still have some hesitation about such a reading, it is due to Pertile's point: to what extent could *Amor che ne la mente* have suggested the full connotations of Filosofia to the early readers of the *Commedia*, who could not have known the context in the *Convivio*?

[7] Robert Hollander, '*Purgatorio* II: Cato's rebuke and Dante's *scoglio*', *Italica*, 52 (1975), 348-63, at p. 348.

[8] Ibid. pp. 348-49.

[9] Ibid. p. 355.

[10] *Dante's Poets* (Princeton, 1984), pp. 38 f.

[11] '*Purgatorio* II: The new song and the old', *Lectura Dantis*, 6 (1990), 28-45, at p. 29. The 'American interpretive position' as expressed by Freccero, on the other hand, is far more finely nuanced (see above, n. 6).

There are many other reasons which render the notion of a rejection of Philosophy in the *Commedia* implausible. As John Scott has valuably reminded us,[12] these include the exaltation of the philosopher Siger of Brabant in the heaven of the Sun, and the homage that Thomas Aquinas pays him there (*Par.* 10, 133-38). They also include the existence of the philosophical treatise *Monarchia*, which, as is now increasingly recognized, must — because of its irrefragable cross-reference, 'as I have already said in the *Paradiso* of the *Comedy*' (*Mon.* I, xii, 6) — belong to the last, maturest period of Dante's thought. In Prue Shaw's words, 'It does not seem too wide of the mark to suggest that the *Monarchia* stands in relation to the *Comedy* as Aristotle's *Politics* stands in relation to his *Ethics* — a text which grows out of an earlier one'.[13] But I should like to put forward one further consideration, which I have not seen mentioned in modern discussions of the Donna Gentile.

In the first redaction of his commentary on the *Commedia* (ca. 1340),[14] Dante's son Pietro, commenting on the 'three blessed ladies' (*tre donne benedette*, *Inf.* 2, 124) who, in the court of heaven, show their concern for Dante's salvation, suggests two interpretations, which he calls, respectively, anagogical and allegorical. The anagogical is quite similar to one found in other early commentators. 'There is a gentle lady in heaven' (*Donna è gentil nel ciel*, *Inf.* 2, 94), who 'breaks the harsh judgement above'; she summons Lucia, who in turn seeks out Beatrice. On this first interpretation, Pietro sees the gentle lady as standing for operating grace, Lucia for co-operating grace, and Beatrice for Theology. His second interpretation (*allegorice*) is more unusual. —

'Philosophy', Pietro here begins, 'is divided principally into three parts: namely natural philosophy, mathematics, and metaphysics or theology'. Soon afterwards he cites, from Boethius' *Consolation of Philosophy* (I pr. 1), the vision of Philosophia, which concludes:

Philosophia now confined herself to the common measure of human beings; now she seemed to touch heaven with the top of her head; and when she lifted her head higher, she penetrated heaven itself and eluded the human gaze.

In these three moments Pietro, by ingenious allegorizing, sees epiphanies of the three blessed ladies. When Philosophia adapts herself to the measure of human contemplation, she is the gentle lady (*domina gentilis*) who is natural philosophy:

Nam nunc ad comunem se hominum mensuram cohibebat: in hoc dicit de parte huius philosophiae naturalis, et haec domina gentilis est, de qua dicitur hic.

[12] J. A. Scott, 'Dante and Philosophy', *Annali d'italianistica*, 8 (1990), 258-77.

[13] Dante, *Monarchia*, ed. and tr. Prue Shaw (Cambridge, 1995), pp. xl-xli (cf. her whole discussion of the dating of the *Monarchia*, pp. xxxviii ff.).

[14] Pietro Alighieri, *Super Dantis ipsius genitoris Comoediam Commentarium*, ed. Vincenzo Nannucci (Florence, 1846), pp. 57-61.

As mathematical science, Philosophia touches heaven: then she is Lucia (*Et haec est Lucia*), whose light is associated with heavenly light and with astronomy. Finally when, in her highest form, metaphysics or theology, Philosophia penetrates heaven itself, then 'it is Beatrice who is spoken of here' (*Et haec est Beatrix, de qua hic dicitur*).

I am not suggesting that Pietro's elaborate philosophical allegory reveals his father's poetic intentions in *Inferno* 2. What we can say for sure, however, in the light of this passage, is that Pietro would have been amazed by the modern notion that his father had rejected the *domina gentilis*, Philosophia, at any time or in any form.